BY ROYAL

MATH ᴇ MAGIC

MAGIC, PUZZLES, AND GAMES WITH NUMBERS

ILLUSTRATED BY GERALD LYNTON KAUFMAN
AND EDITED BY JEROME S. MEYER

DOVER PUBLICATIONS, INC.

The year this book was reissued:

Add any column
Add any row
Add diagonals   } all to be 5 numbers
Add any Grecian Cross
Add any St. Andrew's Cross

Grecian Cross, as

354	397	380	388	404
390	401	386	394	382
396	379	392	403	383
406	385	393	381	389
378	391	402	387	395

St. Andrew's Cross, as.

This Dover edition, first published in 1953, is an unabridged republication of the work originally published by Simon and Schuster, Inc. in 1933.

International Standard Book Number: 0-486-20110-4
Library of Congress Catalog Card Number: 54-1777

Manufactured in the United States of America
Dover Publications, Inc.
31 East 2nd Street, Mineola, N.Y. 11501

FOREWORD

By BERNARD M. L. ERNST

President of the Society of American Magicians
(Parent Assembly)

Throughout the ages men have been interested in mystery and in things that are strange and startling. As in the past, modern magic derives much of its glamor from phenomena which superficially are inexplicable and from the unanticipated results of seemingly normal and commonplace devices and experiments. In recent years so-called "Mathematical Magic" is coming into its own. There are mathematical geniuses and prodigies but these individuals possess inherent gifts which are not possessed by others, and their demonstrations, though startling, are not magic.

Mr. Heath has invented and collected strange things in numbers and in their combination and treatment. He presents in this volume magic mathematical effects which he makes available to all. You select your own digits, he tells you what to do with them, and he announces the result of your own calculations with your own figures. He shows you how you will be surprised in your own treatment of your own numbers. He tells you about many things that can be done by simple "figuring" which are amazing and at first unbelievable.

During the summer of 1929 the author became a member of the Parent Assembly of the Society of American Magicians in New York. After a time a blackboard appeared at every monthly meeting of the assembly and Mr. Heath presented one or more new and original effects in mathematics, all of them as experiments in the "Magic of Numbers." They were so unusual and interesting that he was prevailed upon to publish this book and give many of his ideas to the world. His task has been to select items from his numerous creations and to compress them within the confines of a single volume. His work has been done exceptionally well as the reader will find when he reads the items and puts them into practice.

In these days of mental games and of cross-word and jig-saw puzzles, mathematical magic, long neglected by the general public, should find an enthusiastic response. With it one can entertain oneself and one's friends as well, and, if so inclined, readily build up an "act" for public exhibition and professional profit.

The attractive illustrations in the pages which follow are by Gerald Lynton Kaufman, a well-known New York architect and artist, who is also a member of the Parent Assembly of the Society of American Magicians, and who was so much impressed by Mr. Heath's manipulations with numbers, that artist-like, he simply *had* to make the drawings. Mr. Heath's many friends are already awaiting the publication by him of a supplementary volume with other problems and more of Mr. Kaufman's drawings.

THIS BOOK HAS BEEN APPROVED BY THE COM-MITTEE ON ETHICS AND STANDARDS OF THE SOCIETY OF AMERICAN MAGICIANS AS NOT DETRI-MENTAL TO THE INTERESTS OF THE PROFES-SIONAL MAGICIANS OF AMERICA.

ACKNOWLEDGMENT

The author wishes to acknowledge his indebtedness to Mrs. Clark B. Allen, Bernard M. L. Ernst, Gerald Lynton Kaufman, Jerome S. Meyer, John Mulholland, Robert C. Myles, Jr., and Professor Shirley L. Quimby for the help and encouragement they have given him in the writing of this book.

CONTENTS

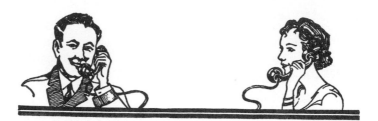

CENTRAL KNOWS YOUR AGE

This is intended to teach you a lesson—that lesson being to keep your telephone number to yourself. Should Central plug in on this trick she'll be able to tell you the age of the person you are calling. It might be slightly embarrassing, should you call some particularly promising number—say, Endicott 9021—and hear Central reply brightly, "You are calling a girl of 24."

Here's how it's worked:

1. Write down the last 4 figures of your telephone number (omitting the number affixed to the central office).
2. Transpose the digits of this number in any way you wish.
3. Subtract the smaller number from the larger. Add up the digits in your result.
4. If you find this total to contain 2 or more digits, keep adding these digits together until you have only 1 digit as a final result.
5. Add 7 to this result.
6. Now add to this total the last 2 digits of the year in which you were born.
7. Subtract 16 from the final result and, lo and behold, out pops the year you were born. Knowing the year of one's birth, moreover, it is easy to find out just how old a person is.

How It Is Done

It just happens that when you take any number (regardless of the number of digits), transpose it and subtract the smaller from the larger, the resulting numbers add up to 9 or to multiples of 9. It is obvious that if you keep adding them together they will eventually be reduced to one number, *that number must be 9*. If you add 7 to this 9 and subsequently remove 16 (which you just did) the result is obviously zero. This zero plus the last 2 digits of the year in which you were born gives away your birth year— or your age on or before December 31st of the current year.

Let's take an example. If anyone cares to, he can reach me at Columbus 0340. With hardly anything up my sleeve I scrambled the number as follows: 4300. Subtracting the smaller number from the larger, I find myself with 3960 in my hands. Adding these I get 18, which when added again gives me 9. Now I add 7 and the last 2 figures of the year of my birth (1895)—or 95, and I get 16 plus 95 = 111.

Removing the pesky 16, the final result is 95. Therefore you may assume that I am now 58, which is quite correct.

Once you are convinced that this trick works try it on someone else, emphasizing heavily the mystic powers with which employees of your local telephone company have endowed you.

THE ROBBER AND THE SHEEP

Here is a particularly good one to spring on your friends as you dine. It is best when worked while you are all waiting for the soup, or after you have finished your demi-tasse.

When the waiter isn't watching you, sneak 7 lumps of sugar out of the bowl. Arrange these 7 pieces in front of you as follows:

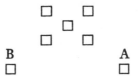

Now, if your hands are clean—and they should be if you are dining out with your friends—expose them, palms upward. Explain that you have a story to tell, and that in this story your hands play the part of empty barns.

Now pick up the piece of sugar marked A in your right hand, and announce that A is a robber who goes into the right-hand barn.

Then with your left hand, pick up the piece of sugar marked B, affirming that this is another robber who goes into the left barn.

From now on keep both hands closed in fist fashion.

9

Now explain that the remaining 5 pieces of sugar are 5 sheep, which each robber sees from his respective barn. Since the coast is clear, Robber A (right hand) sneaks up and steals one sheep. (*Take one of the pieces of sugar in your right fist.*)

Robber B, seeing how easy it is, does the same. (*Take another piece of sugar in your left fist.*)

Robber A now steals another sheep, and so does Robber B. This leaves one sheep on the table which Robber A (right hand) steals. *Your right fist now contains 4 pieces of sugar, and your left fist 3.*

Holding your fist closed tight, announce dramatically that a shepherd is approaching. The robbers, peering out from their respective barns, decide to return the sheep to prevent being caught wool-gathering.

In returning the sheep to the original places, *start with the left fist first, then the right, then the left, then the right, then the left.* Now all 5 sheep have been replaced on the table—just where they were originally, but, *if you have followed closely, you will see that you now have nothing in your left fist, and 2 pieces of sugar in your right. Of course, your friends don't know this. They think you have a piece of sugar in each fist.*

Your story continues somewhat in this fashion: "The shepherd crosses the field and, seeing all the sheep in their proper places, goes on about his business. As soon as the coast is again clear, the robbers decide to steal the sheep all over again."

Now, repeat your initial actions: Start with your right fist and pick up a piece of sugar; then follow with the left fist, then the right again, then the left, and, finally, the right. *You now have 5 pieces in your right fist and only 2 in your left.*

At this point, tell your audience that the shepherd is returning with the village constable.

The robbers, in their respective barns, are considerably harassed. They know they will be caught, since it is too late to return the sheep. Consequently, they decide that the only way out is for them both to be found asleep in one barn, and the 5 sheep safely picketed in the other. If this could be accomplished, there would be no evidence against them.

Now announce proudly that the robbers found the way out. Open your right hand, showing the 5 sheep safe in the one barn. Open your left hand, showing the 2 robbers sound asleep and comfy in the other.

This is really a swell trick, but be sure *to pick up the sheep with the right hand first, and to return them to the fold, starting with the left hand.*

Need we say that this will make your audience look sheepish indeed.

FAMILY HISTRICK

Here's a trick to practice on "his sisters and his cousins and his aunts," together with future in-laws. It works best, however, with brothers or sisters.

Here's what you do: Ask a brother or a sister to:

1. Write down the number of brothers he or she has living.
2. Multiply by 2.
3. Add 3.
4. Multiply this number by 5.
5. Add to this the number of living sisters.
6. Multiply the total by 10.
7. Add the number of dead brothers and dead sisters.
8. Now look squarely at your victim and demand the answer.
9. When he tells you the answer, subtract 150 from it and the first digit on the left-hand side of your result tells you the number of his living brothers; the middle digit gives you the number of his living sisters and the right-hand digit tells you the number of his dead brothers and sisters.

12

How It Works Out

Suppose Nellie had 2 living brothers, 3 sisters who are quite alive and 4 dead brothers and sisters:

Then she writes down the following according to rule:

		2	living brothers
2nd step:	×	2	
		4	
3rd step:	plus	3	
		7	
4th step:	×	5	
		35	
5th step:	plus	3	living sisters
		38	
6th step:	×	10	
		380	
7th step:	plus	4	dead brothers and sisters
		384	
		150	subtracted
		234	

Answer: 234

Left-hand digit — 2 — living brothers
Middle digit — 3 — living sisters
Right-hand digit — 4 — dead brothers and sisters

THE LIE DETECTOR

Try this trick on males first. We won't guarantee your popularity with the fair sex unless you use tact and discretion. If, for example, you find that your girl friend has chopped off a few years from her age (which often happens in the best-regulated girls) tell her she told the truth and watch her lap it up. If you ever have a row with her you can always prove you knew she lied about her age—and just how much.

Some girls will naturally lie about their age. Therefore, if you do this trick in mixed company you are sure to catch someone off guard. For this reason it is best that your victim does not know that you can detect lies. It is ever so much more fun to say to Flo after she has answered your questions: "It's safe with me." If she wants to know how much she lied—tell her! But make sure she really wants to know.

This trick is so simple a ten-year-old child can do it. You can be an expert lie detector in less than five minutes.

Column 1 tells you what to ask your victims. Column 2 shows you what goes on in their minds (or on the paper you give them but don't see) and column 3 shows what happens when they lie.

What to Tell Your Victim to Do	The Truth *SAM is 27*	A Lie *FLO is 29*
1. Write down your age (up to the end of this year). Don't tell it to me.	Sam writes 27	Flo writes 22
2. Add to this your age next year.	Sam adds 27 28 —— 55	Flo adds 22 23 —— 45
3. Multiply by 5.	Sam multiplies $5 \times 55 = 275$	Flo multiplies $5 \times 45 = 225$
4. Now say quickly: "Of course you know the year you were born— add the last digit of this year to your result."	Sam figures he was born in 1926 so he adds 6 to 275	Flo, taken off her guard, knows she was born in 1924 but, feeling that the last digit can't give her away, adds 4 to 225
5. Ask Sam and Flo for their results.	Sam announces 281	Flo announces 229

Take Sam first: Deduct 5 from 281 = 276 and note the first 2 digits (27) which is the age Sam wrote down. Now subtract the remaining digit (6) from the last digit of this year (1953) and you have

$$\begin{array}{r} 1953 \\ -6 \\ \hline 7 \end{array}$$

15

This 7 and the 7 of 27 are the same. That means Sam told the truth.

Now take Flo: Do the same with Flo. Subtract 5 from her 229 = 224. Note the first 2 digits 22 which is the age Flo gave herself. Now take the last digit (4) from the last digit of 1933 and you get

$$\begin{array}{r} 1953 \\ -4 \\ \hline 9 \end{array}$$

This 9 represents the second digit in her true age. As this 9 and the 2 of the 22 do not agree, we know Flo lied. She said she was 22 and she is really 29. Deceptive Flo!

Now let us summarize this trick step by step.

1. Write down your present age (up to the end of this year).
2. Add to this your age next year.
3. Multiply by 5.
4. Add the last digit of the year of your birth.
5. Tell me the result.

When you hear this number deduct 5 from it. The result will always be a number of three digits, the first two of which give you the age your friend wrote down.

To find out whether or not he told the truth merely subtract the third digit from the last two digits of the present year ('53) and consider the last figure only. For example, after deducting 5 from the number Sam gave you, you have 276. You know instantly that he said he was 27 and if you deduct the 6 from 53 and consider the last digit only of this answer, you'll have 7. Compare this with the last number of his age—if it corresponds your friend told the truth. In this case he did. If, in the case of Flo, the final number does not correspond to the last digit of her age, you'll know your friend did not tell the truth. You will also know how much he or she lied.

ARITHMENTAL WHOOPEE

This trick illustrates an old East Indian theory—that the things which apparently appear most baffling are really the easiest to learn and to do. For example:

On a scrap of paper, write down any number between 1 and 50. Fold the paper. Hand it to a friend and tell him to put it in his pocket without looking at it. Now give him some paper and ask him to write down any number between 50 and 100, without letting you see it. Then tell him to add to the number he wrote down, a number which you will give him. When he has done this, tell him to cross out the first left-hand figure in his total, add it to the remaining number, and, finally, to subtract the result from the number he originally wrote down.

Now tell him to look at the folded paper you gave him, and he will see that the figure on it tallies with his result. Let's go behind the scenes:

17

What You Do	What Your Friend Does
1. You write down any number less than 99 (say 23) on a piece of paper; fold it, and hand it to your friend, telling him not to look at it.	He slips the paper into his pocket without looking at it.
2. Tell him to write down any number between 50 and 100 without letting you see it.	He writes 86.

3. You subtract the number you wrote on the piece of paper (23) from 99 mentally, and tell your friend to add 76 to his number.	He adds: 86
	   76
	   ─────
	  162

4. Tell him to cross off the first number and add it to the result.	He does so: 1̸62
	      1
	   ─────
	   63

5. Now tell him to subtract his result from the original number and look at the folded piece of paper you gave him.	He subtracts: 86
	   63
	   ─────
	   23

He looks at the folded paper and sees the number 23. He is, we trust, stupefied.

Of course, this trick can be worked with higher numbers, too. You can ask the victim to write down any number between 200 and 1,000. In this case, the number you write on the folded paper must be between 100 and 200, and the number you subtract from in the third step must be 999, instead of 99.

What You Do	**What Your Friend Does**
1. You write down 143 on a piece of paper, fold it and give it to your friend, telling him not to look at it.	Your friend puts it in his pocket without looking at it.
2. Tell him to write down any number between 200 and 1,000.	He writes 493.
3. Subtract the number you wrote on the folded paper (143) from 999 and tell your friend to add 856 to his number.	He adds: 493 856 ――― 1349
4. Tell him to cross off the first digit and add it to the result.	He does so: 1̸349 1 ――― 350
5. Ask him to subtract this result from his original number.	He subtracts: 493 350 ――― 143

He now compares this with the number you wrote on the piece of paper in his pocket.

By the same method this trick can be done for numbers between 300,000 and 1,000,000.

The identical arithmetical principle also enables you to tell any-one's age provided he or she is more than 10 years old. Just tell your friend to add 90 to his age, cross off the first digit of his result and add it to the remaining two digits. When he tells you his answer merely add 9 and tell him his age.

Suppose your friend is 26
He adds 90
                                          ——
                                          116
He crosses off the first .... 𝟣̶16
figure and adds 1
                                          ——
                                          17

When he tells you 17, you add 9 and tell him he is 26.

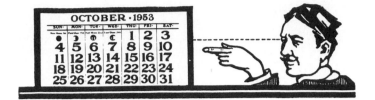

AN EVENTRIC

Let's suppose that you are throwing a great big party with lots of people who are willing to be astonished. From this point on you conduct yourself in the following manner:

1. Ask someone to write down the year of his birth and, under that, the year of some great event in his life, such as the time he saved the banker's daughter from the runaway horse.
2. Now tell him to write down the number of people in the room.
3. Suggest that he write down his age.
4. Ask him to jot down the number of years ago that the great event in his life took place.
5. Now tell him to add these figures all together. At this point you confound him by telling him the total.

Explanation

The year of anyone's birth plus his age always equals the present year (1953). The year of a great event plus the number of years ago that it happened also must always equal the present year. Obviously, if you add both of these together you get 2 × 1953 or 3906.

21

Now you will find that there is but one more item on the list, the number of people in the room. You know that figure. To get the total, therefore, all you need do is add the number of people in the room at the time to 3906 (twice (1953).

A Typical Example

Suppose one was born in.................... 1890
Suppose the big event took place in........... 1921
Suppose there are 6 people in the room........   6
*Therefore his age is...................... 63
The great event occurred 32 years ago........ 32
                                          _____
                                             3912

All you do is take your static number, 3906 (which is twice 1953), and add the number of persons in the room—6. This of course gives you that same darn 3912.

Here's a pleasant variation on this trick: Suppose there are 8 people in the room. You now take a deck of cards and choose from it a 3, 8, 7 and 4. This, of course, represents 3866 plus the 8 people in the room—3874. Place these 4 cards at the bottom of the deck. Now work the trick exactly as above and ask for the total. When this total is revealed you proceed to deal the pack into four stacks. When the deal is completed the 3, 8, 7 and 4 will top each stack. Accompanying your actions with the patter common to workers of magic you go through the trick and finally expose the top card of each pile. When people ask you how the trick is worked don't tell them.

---

* It is important that the victim write down his age as of December 31st of the current year. That is, if John is 23 now but will be 24 in October he writes down 24 when you ask him for his age. Keep this point clear in your mind.

I'M TELLIN' YOU

Here is a little stunt which you can work along with your friends.

1. Take any number at all.
2. Now add the number next higher in sequence.
3. Add 9 to that result.
4. Divide by 2.
5. Now subtract your original number.

The answer will always be 5.

Here's the way it works out:

Suppose you write down....................	597
Now you add.............................	598
	1195
Now add	9
	1204
Divide by 2..............................	602
Subtract	597
Answer	5

If you have already worked this trick and want to repeat it in more modern dress, tell your audience to add any odd number as the third step. If you ask them to add 11, their final answer will always be 6. If you request that they add 13, the answer must be 7.

Here's another way of phrasing it. Every odd number added to the first total always results in that number plus 1, divided by 2.

Add	3	5	7	9	11	13	15	17	19	21	23	
Answer	2	3	4	5	6	7	8	9	10	11	12	etc.

THE DIME AND THE PENNY

In the good old days, folks used to play this one with a one dollar bill and a ten spot. Now it is played with a dime and a penny.

Granting that you can scrape 11c together, turn it over to a trustworthy friend to hold for you.

Tell him to put the dime in one hand and the penny in the other.

Ask him to multiply the value of the coin in his right hand by 4, 6 or 8, and the value of the coin in his left hand by 3, 5 or 7.

Now ask him to add the results and tell you the total. If the total is *even*, he has the penny in his right hand; if the total is *odd*, he has it in his left.

There's another variation for folks who are only able to produce a penny and a nickel.

Tell the victim to place one coin in each hand.

Then say: "Multiply whatever is in your right hand by 14."

When he says "O. K.," or words to that effect, say: "Now, multiply the coin in your left hand by 14."

Ask him to add the two sums and, without waiting for the result, tell him in which hands the coins are. This will be simple for you, since you can easily judge the time it takes to multiply by 14. The penny, of course, can be multiplied mentally immediately, while you will note some hesitation on his part when he tries to multiply 5 by 14.

Sounds silly, of course, but you'll be surprised by the results you get.

CHILD'S PLAY

Some day when conversation lags and you find yourself with nothing to talk about, produce a pencil and paper, hand them to a friend, and ask him to write down any number between 3 and 10. Now tell him to proceed as follows:

1. Add 5 to this number and write the result to the right of the original number.
2. Multiply the first number by itself.
3. Multiply the second number, or numbers, by itself or themselves.
4. Add these two totals together and multiply the result by 2.

Now ask your friend for his answer and tell him the two numbers he thought of originally.

In order to find out the two numbers he was thinking of, here's what you do:

1. Subtract 25 from his result.
2. Take the square root of the resulting number.
3. Subtract 5.
4. Divide by 2—and you'll have his first number; add 5— and you'll get his second number.

For example: Suppose your friend originally took the number 6.

He adds 5 to 6 and writes down the number 11 to the right of number 6.

He now squares the first number, and gets 36.

He squares the second number, and gets 121.

He adds them together and gets 157.

He multiplies by 2 and gets 314, which is the number he tells you.

You deduct 25 from 314, and get 289.

Taking the square root of 289, you get 17.

You subtract 5 from 17, and you get 12.

You divide 12 by 2 and you arrive at his first number, 6.

As you know, the difference between his first and second number was 5. Therefore, you merely add 5, which gives you 11, or his second number.

Of course this principle can be used with *any* difference between the numbers.

MORE CHILD'S PLAY

1. Take any number of two digits.
2. Add 6 to it, and place the result to the right.
3. Multiply each of the two numbers by themselves, and subtract the lesser total from the greater.
4. Tell me the result, and I'll tell you both original numbers.

Suppose 63 is selected as the original number.

Increasing this by 6, we get 69.

Now, squaring both numbers, we have:

$$\begin{array}{r} 63 \\ 63 \\ \hline 189 \\ 378 \\ \hline 3969 \end{array} \qquad \begin{array}{r} 69 \\ 69 \\ \hline 621 \\ 414 \\ \hline 4761 \end{array}$$

Subtracting the lesser from the greater, we get:

$$\begin{array}{r} 4761 \\ 3969 \\ \hline 792 \end{array}$$

Here's what you do: Take the number 6, which was added to the original number.

Multiply this by 2, which gives you 12.

Divide the total your friend gives you by 12.

Dividing 792 by 12, you get 66.

Adding and subtracting one-half of 6 to 66 gives us the two original numbers, 63 and 69.

In step two above, you asked your friend to add 6 to his first number. It is possible to work this trick with *any* number. Thus, if he adds 8, the trick can also be worked. All you do later is to multiply this number by 2 and divide it into the result which your friend passes on to you. When you have found the final result, add and subtract to it one-half of the number used in step two.

A-NUMGRAM

Just in case you're an anagram fan, this little trick was conceived to send off the game to a flying start.

Before you begin to play, pick out six letters.

Write a number on the back of each letter as follows:

Take the letters: G L O R I A
On the reverse side of G place the number 16
On the reverse side of L place the number 13
On the reverse side of O place the number 49
On the reverse side of R place the number 85
On the reverse side of I place the number 98
On the reverse side of A place the number 77

Place the six letters on the table letter face up.

Turn your back and ask someone present to note the number on the back of any letter.

Tell him to replace this letter and shuffle it among the other five.

Now produce a pencil from your pocket and tell your audience that you are going to tap on some of the letters. Ask your friend to spell out *his* number, letting each tap you make represent a letter in the spelling of his selected number.

Advise him that when his number has been spelled out by your taps, he is to stop you and when he has stopped you, your pencil will be resting on the number he selected. For example, if his selection were the number 85 (as E-I-G-H-T-Y F-I-V-E has ten letters), he must stop you on the 10th tap and your pencil will then be resting on that numgram.

Here's How It Works

Take your pencil and tap on *any* letters for the first six taps, but be sure on the seventh tap to tap the letter "G." On the eighth tap the letter "L," on the ninth tap to tap the letter "O," etc., and no matter what number was selected you will be right because:

SIXTEEN	(on the back of the letter G) has	7 letters
THIRTEEN	(on the back of the letter L) has	8 letters
FORTY-NINE	(on the back of the letter O) has	9 letters
EIGHTY-FIVE	(on the back of the letter R) has	10 letters
NINETY-EIGHT	(on the back of the letter I) has	11 letters
SEVENTY-SEVEN	(on the back of the letter A) has	12 letters

In the next section you will find some gorgeous number patterns—each pattern having its own particular motif and theme just as though it were a symphony in numbers. We ask you to consider in particular the two mystic numbers. They're quite amazing.

A close study of these numerical arrangements will begin to reveal to you some of the inexhaustible logical oddities which result from the simple fact that ours is a decimal system of counting.

32

A SYMPHONY IN FRACTIONS

$$11 \times 11 = 121$$
$$111 \times 111 = 12321$$
$$1111 \times 1111 = 1234321$$
$$11111 \times 11111 = 123454321$$
$$111111 \times 111111 = 12345654321$$
$$1111111 \times 1111111 = 1234567654321$$
$$11111111 \times 11111111 = 123456787654321$$
$$111111111 \times 111111111 = 12345678987654321$$

NOTE
The denominator of the fraction has the same digits as the whole number with plus signs between.

NOTE
The digits in the numerator of the fraction are the same as the middle digit of the whole number and there are as many digits in the numerator as the middle digit of the whole number indicates.

$$121 = \frac{22 \times 22}{1+2+1}$$

$$12321 = \frac{333 \times 333}{1+2+3+2+1}$$

$$1234321 = \frac{4444 \times 4444}{1+2+3+4+3+2+1}$$

$$123454321 = \frac{55555 \times 55555}{1+2+3+4+5+4+3+2+1}$$

$$12345654321 = \frac{666666 \times 666666}{1+2+3+4+5+6+5+4+3+2+1}$$

$$1234567654321 = \frac{7777777 \times 7777777}{1+2+3+4+5+6+7+6+5+4+3+2+1}$$

$$123456787654321 = \frac{88888888 \times 88888888}{1+2+3+4+5+6+7+8+7+6+5+4+3+2+1}$$

$$12345678987654321 = \frac{999999999 \times 999999999}{1+2+3+4+5+6+7+8+9+8+7+6+5+4+3+2+1}$$

33

THE MYSTIC NUMBER 76923

$76923 \times 1 = 076923$

$76923 \times 10 = 769230$

$76923 \times 9 = 692307$

$76923 \times 12 = 923076$

$76923 \times 3 = 230769$

$76923 \times 4 = 307692$

NOTE

The number 76923, when multiplied by 1, 10, 9, 12, 3 and 4 gives the same sequence of digits read up and down and across. Every row and every column adds up to 27. Note all the diagonals in the ↙ direction are the same numbers.

The same number 76923, when multiplied by 2, 7, 5, 11, 6 and 8 gives the same sequence of digits, namely 153846 read up and down and across. Every row and column adds up to 27. Note all the diagonals in the direction ↙ are the same numbers.

$76923 \times 2 = 153846$

$76923 \times 7 = 538461$

$76923 \times 5 = 384615$

$76923 \times 11 = 846153$

$76923 \times 6 = 461538$

$76923 \times 8 = 615384$

34

THE MAGIC NUMBER 142857

$$111111 = 7 \times 15873$$
$$222222 = 7 \times 31746$$
$$333333 = 7 \times 47619$$
$$444444 = 7 \times 63492$$
$$555555 = 7 \times 79365$$
$$666666 = 7 \times 95328$$
$$777777 = 7 \times 111111$$
$$888888 = 7 \times 126984$$
$$999999 = 7 \times \underline{142857}$$

NOTE
When all the numbers containing the digits 142857 are multiplied by 7, we get five columns of 9s and the first and last columns add up to 9.

$$142857 \times 1 = 142857 \times 7 = 0999999 \div 9$$
$$142857 \times 3 = 428571 \times 7 = 2999997 \div 9$$
$$142857 \times 2 = 285714 \times 7 = 1999998 \div 9$$
$$142857 \times 6 = 857142 \times 7 = 5999994 \div 9$$
$$142857 \times 4 = 571428 \times 7 = 3999996 \div 9$$
$$142857 \times 5 = 714285 \times 7 = 4999995 \div 9$$

The number 142857, when multiplied by 1, 3, 2, 6, 4 and 5 gives the same sequence of digits read up and down and across. Every row and every column add up to 27—just the same as the mystic number 76923. All diagonals in the ⟋ direction, are the same numbers.

$$111111 = 3 \times 37037$$
$$33333 = 9 \times 37037$$
$$22222 = 6 \times 37037$$
$$666666 = 18 \times 37037$$
$$444444 = 12 \times 37037$$
$$555555 = 15 \times 37037$$

1089 AND ALL THAT

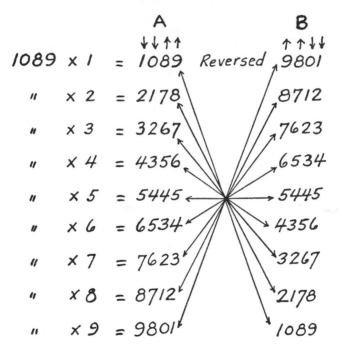

	A	B
	↓↓↑↑	↑↑↓↓
1089 × 1 =	1089 Reversed	9801
" × 2 =	2178	8712
" × 3 =	3267	7623
" × 4 =	4356	6534
" × 5 =	5445	5445
" × 6 =	6534	4356
" × 7 =	7623	3267
" × 8 =	8712	2178
" × 9 =	9801	1089

NOTE
The 1st column in A increases from top to bottom consecutively. The second column does the same. The 3rd and 4th column decreases from top to bottom consecutively. The figures in column B are just the reverse of column A. Note also that column B is column A in reverse order.

36

YOU'D NEVER THINK IT OF 19 AND 9109

```
19 × 1 = 19 and 1+9 = 10 and 1+0 = 1
19 × 2 = 38  "  3+8 = 11   "  1+1 = 2
19 × 3 = 57  "  5+7 = 12   "  1+2 = 3
19 × 4 = 76  "  7+6 = 13   "  1+3 = 4
19 × 5 = 95  "  9+5 = 14   "  1+4 = 5
19 × 6 = 114 "  11+4 = 15  "  1+5 = 6
19 × 7 = 133 "  13+3 = 16  "  1+6 = 7
19 × 8 = 152 "  15+2 = 17  "  1+7 = 8
19 × 9 = 171 "  17+1 = 18  "  1+8 = 9
19 × 10 = 190 " 19+0 = 19  "  1+9 = 10
```

```
              ↓  ↑  ↓  ↓  ↑
9109 × 1 =    0  9  1  0  9  add digits =  19
9109 × 2 =    1  8  2  1  8    "     "   = 20
9109 × 3 =    2  7  3  2  7    "     "   = 21
9109 × 4 =    3  6  4  3  6    "     "   = 22
9109 × 5 =    4  5  5  4  5    "     "   = 23
9109 × 6 =    5  4  6  5  4    "     "   = 24
9109 × 7 =    6  3  7  6  3    "     "   = 25
9109 × 8 =    7  2  8  7  2    "     "   = 26
9109 × 9 =    8  1  9  8  1    "     "   = 27
```

Note how these columns
run from 1 to 9 and from
9 to 1.

37

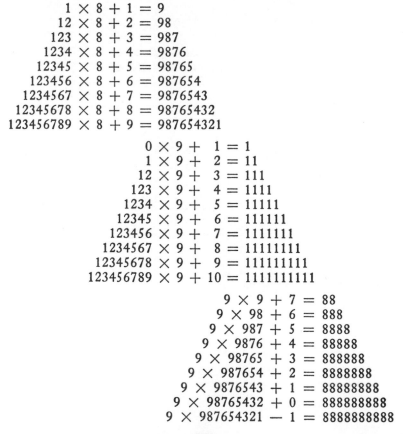

NUMBER SYMPHONIES

SOME PRETTY ARRANGEMENTS

$$1 \times 8 + 1 = 9$$
$$12 \times 8 + 2 = 98$$
$$123 \times 8 + 3 = 987$$
$$1234 \times 8 + 4 = 9876$$
$$12345 \times 8 + 5 = 98765$$
$$123456 \times 8 + 6 = 987654$$
$$1234567 \times 8 + 7 = 9876543$$
$$12345678 \times 8 + 8 = 98765432$$
$$123456789 \times 8 + 9 = 987654321$$

$$0 \times 9 + 1 = 1$$
$$1 \times 9 + 2 = 11$$
$$12 \times 9 + 3 = 111$$
$$123 \times 9 + 4 = 1111$$
$$1234 \times 9 + 5 = 11111$$
$$12345 \times 9 + 6 = 111111$$
$$123456 \times 9 + 7 = 1111111$$
$$1234567 \times 9 + 8 = 11111111$$
$$12345678 \times 9 + 9 = 111111111$$
$$123456789 \times 9 + 10 = 1111111111$$

$$9 \times 9 + 7 = 88$$
$$9 \times 98 + 6 = 888$$
$$9 \times 987 + 5 = 8888$$
$$9 \times 9876 + 4 = 88888$$
$$9 \times 98765 + 3 = 888888$$
$$9 \times 987654 + 2 = 8888888$$
$$9 \times 9876543 + 1 = 88888888$$
$$9 \times 98765432 + 0 = 888888888$$
$$9 \times 987654321 - 1 = 8888888888$$

ALL THE SAME NUMBER

$$12345679 \times 9 = 111\ 111\ 111$$
$$12345679 \times 18 = 222\ 222\ 222$$
$$12345679 \times 27 = 333\ 333\ 333$$
$$12345679 \times 36 = 444\ 444\ 444$$
$$12345679 \times 45 = 555\ 555\ 555$$
$$12345679 \times 54 = 666\ 666\ 666$$
$$12345679 \times 63 = 777\ 777\ 777$$
$$12345679 \times 72 = 888\ 888\ 888$$
$$12345679 \times 81 = 999\ 999\ 999$$

$$1+2+1 = 2^2$$
$$1+2+3+2+1 = 3^2$$
$$1+2+3+4+3+2+1 = 4^2$$
$$1+2+3+4+5+4+3+2+1 = 5^2$$
$$1+2+3+4+5+6+5+4+3+2+1 = 6^2$$
$$1+2+3+4+5+6+7+6+5+4+3+2+1 = 7^2$$
$$1+2+3+4+5+6+7+8+7+6+5+4+3+2+1 = 8^2$$
$$1+2+3+4+5+6+7+8+9+8+7+6+5+4+3+2+1 = 9^2$$

Notice relationship of the above with the denominators of the symphony in fractions on page 38.

EASY WAYS TO MULTIPLY

Perhaps you have seen lightning calculators in action and have been impressed by them. This section of the book is intended to show you how the trick's done. You will find in these pages how to multiply two figures by two more figures within the brief span of five seconds.

The systems set forth in this chapter have no connection with magic. They are carefully worked out, efficient time-savers. Perhaps they will even help you to solve practical every-day problems, both in business and social life.

Let us begin with a quick way to multiply two digits by two others mentally. Before illustrating this with numbers, let us set forth the principle which underlies it.

1. Multiply the last figure of both numbers (carry over what is necessary).

2. Multiply the first digit of the first number by the last digit of the second number, and add the number carried over from the first step, if any.

3. Multiply the first digit of the second number by the last digit of the first number, and add results. Put down the last figure and carry whatever necessary.

4. Multiply the first digit of the first number by the first digit of the second number. Add what you have carried and put down the result.

40

Now let us do this step by step numerically:

$$\begin{array}{r} 64 \\ \times\ 28 \end{array}$$

$8 \times 4 = 32$; put down 2 and carry 3, thus:

$$\begin{array}{r} 64 \\ 28 \\ \hline 2 \end{array}$$

$$\begin{array}{r} 8 \times 6 = 48 \\ 2 \times 4 = 8 \\ \hline 56 + 3 = 59; \text{ put down 9 and} \\ \text{carry 5, thus:} \end{array}$$

$$\begin{array}{r} 64 \\ 28 \\ \hline 92 \end{array}$$

$$\begin{array}{r} 64 \\ 28 \end{array} \qquad \begin{array}{r} 64 \\ 28 \end{array}$$

$2 \times 6 = 12 + 5 = 17$; put down the 17, thus: 1792

The principle can be illustrated by the following diagram. The arrows mean multiplication.

Now examine this example and practice some others for yourself.

```
  38
× 13
```

1st step: $3 \times 8 = 24$
put down 4
carry 2

2nd step: $3 \times 3 = 9$
$1 \times 8 = 8$
17 add the
$2 = 19$

put down 9
carry 1

3rd step: $3 \times 1 = 3$ add the
$1 = 4$ 4   Answer: 494

The same general principle can be applied to multiplying three digits by two digits or three digits by three digits. The following diagrams will serve to illustrate the method of operation. Remember a line connecting two dots means multiplying those dots.

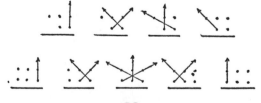

If you practice this for a while you will become proficient and it will not be very long before you will get the knack and be able to do similar problems without pencil and paper, quickly and accurately.

To multiply three digits by two digits:

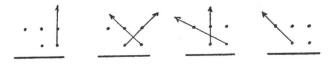

To square any two digit number ending in 5:

Merely add 1 to the lower first digit and use the result to multiply the upper first digit. Annex a 25 ($5 \times 5 = 25$). For example:

$$45$$
$$45$$

add 1 to 4 = 5
$5 \times 4 = 20$
Annex 25, and we get 2025

$$35$$
$$35$$

add 1 to 3 = 4
$4 \times 3 = 12$
Annex 25, and we get 1225

43

To multiply two digits by two digits when the first digit is the same in both numbers and the sum of the last digits equals 10:

Merely multiply the last two digits, put the result down, add 1 to one of the first digits and multiply it by the other digit. Put the result down. Examples:

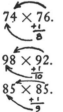

74×76. Put down 24 (6×4), add 1 to one of the 7's and multiply it by the other 7. Answer: 5,624.

98×92. Put down 16. Add 1 to 9 and multiply the answer, 10, by 9. Answer: 9,016.

85×85. Put down 25. Add 1 to 8 and multiply the answer, 9, by 8. Answer: 7,225.

This principle also applies when the two digits in the first number are the same and the two digits in the second number add up to 10. But in your second step, the 1 must always be added to the first digit of the multiplier.

For example:

$$88$$
$$64$$

$$6 + 1 = 7 \text{ and } 7 \times 8 = 56$$
$$4 \times 8 = \quad 32$$
$$\text{Answer } \overline{5632}$$

44

THE LOST DIGIT

Did you ever lose a digit? It's a terrible feeling—especially when it is lost from a number of four figures. You just don't know where to look for it. But if your friend loses one and won't tell you what digit it is, it's easy for you to locate it. Here's how you do it.

Tell your friend to write down a 4 digit number. Don't let him show you what he wrote.

When he has done that, ask him to put the sum of these 4 digits to the right.

Now tell him to cross out 1 of the 4 *original* digits and write the 3 remaining ones above the sum of the digits (which he placed to the right). Then ask him to subtract one from the other and tell you his result.

When you hear this answer, you add up the digits mentally and subtract the sum from the nearest multiple of 9—this gives you the digit he crossed out.

Here is a bird's-eye view of what happens:

What You Say	What He Does
1. Write down a 4-figure number.	He writes 7128.
2. Add up the digits and place your answer to the *right*.	He adds and writes 18.
3. Now cross out any one of the original 4 digits.	He crosses off the 1, thus: 7̸128.
4. Write the remaining 3 digits above the sum you found.	He writes 728 over 18, thus: 728 18
5. Subtract one- from the other.	He subtracts and gets 710
6 Tell your result.	He tells you 710.

As soon as you hear this number, add the digits and you get 8. Subtract this 8 from the nearest multiple of 9 (which in this example is 9), and you get 1, or the number crossed out. It's really very simple—try it with any 4-figure number. If the result given to you happens to add up to 9 or 18, the number crossed out is either a 9 or a zero. In this rare case you will have to guess. You can say: "It is either a 9 or a zero" and your friend will still be willing to admit that you have his number.

THE COO-COO CALCULATOR

Elmer is a most eccentric fellow. He left school when he was only 9, and has since developed a peculiar antipathy to education. He learned how to add numbers, but never discovered how fractions were worked. He boasts that he can multiply or divide any number at all—by 2—but unfortunately he can't multiply or divide by any other number.

Offhand, you'd think this would be a serious handicap. It would be to anyone but Elmer. I might add that Elmer also hates all even numbers. Whenever he sees them, he crosses them out.

Recently, he ran head-on into a simple multiplication problem. Knowing Elmer's very limited knowledge of arithmetic, I felt sorry for him. I tried to help him, but he wouldn't let me. He insisted on working it his own way, and here's how he did it.

To Multiply 39 × 42

He divided 39 by 2. "It's 19," he said, peering up at me.

"No," I replied, "it's 19½."

"I don't know anything about fractions," he said, and wrote down 19.

47

"19 divided by 2 is 9," he remarked a moment later.

"You are wrong again," I insisted, "it's 9½."

"I told you I had never studied fractions," he retorted, and wrote down 9.

He continued dividing by 2 and got the numbers 4, 2 and 1.

Then he turned his attention to the figure 42, and started to multiply by 2 in this fashion:

$$2 \times 42 = 84$$
$$2 \times 84 = 168$$
$$2 \times 168 = 336$$
and so on.

He then arranged his work neatly enough as follows:

	39 ×	42	
divide by 2 each time	19 ×	84	*multiply by 2 each time*
	9 ×	168	
(omit fractions)	~~4 × 336~~		
	~~2 × 672~~		
	1 ×	1344	
		1638	

He ran his eye up and down, seeking each even number in the left-hand column which he immediately crossed out, together with the number directly opposite it as above.

Then he added the remaining figures in the right-hand column and got 1638.

"That's the way I work it," he said proudly, handing me his paper.

Elmer may not be particularly bright; still 39 × 42 *is* 1638. And the funny part about it is that Elmer's system works with any number, no matter how many digits it contains.

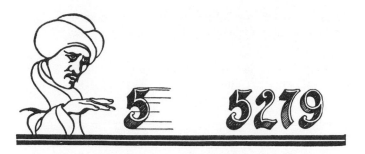

DIGITELLUS

In this brain-twister, your patient writes down any number of four digits and, a moment later, you reveal what number he was thinking of.

Ask him to write down any year in modern history, or the year in which he was born, or any four-digit 'phone number.

In the left column below are the remarks you make. At the right are facts which he writes down on a piece of paper, which must always be concealed from your view. Here is a bird's-eye view of the entire process:

What You Say	**What He Does**
1. Write down any number of four digits, without letting me see the number.	Suppose he chooses 1895.
2. Write down the first two digits.	He writes down: 18
3. Add to these first two digits the number next higher in sequence.	He adds: 18 19 ――― 37
4. Multiply this by 5.	He multiplies $37 \times 5 = 185$.

5. Place a zero at the right of your total in order to make this a four-digit number.

He puts the zero after 185, making 1850.

6. Now give me any number between 10 and 99, and add it to the four-digit number you just arrived at.

He mentions 27 and adds it to 1850:

$$\begin{array}{r} 1850 \\ 27 \\ \hline 1877 \end{array}$$

7. Add to this total the last two digits of the original number you wrote down, and tell me the result.

He adds 95 to 1877, and tells you 1972.

When you hear this number, subtract 50 plus the number he told you in step No. 6 (27 in this case), *and you have his number:*

$$\begin{array}{r} 1972 \\ 77 \\ \hline 1895 \end{array}$$

When you get to be an expert at this trick, you'll eventually be able to work it with money. If you happen to have a friend who goes around with more than $10 in his pocket you will be able to tell him exactly how much money he has with him. You'll also be able to "guess" the price he paid for this or that without his knowing how you do it.

DICE-CYPHERING

Should you ever want to break up a backgammon, parchesi or crap game, just turn your back and tell one of the players to toss the dice. Then ask him to follow these instructions:

1. Write down the number which shows uppermost on the first die.
2. Multiply that number by 2, and add 1.
3. Now multiply by 5.
4. Add the number of the second die.
5. Announce the result.

When he tells you the result, all you have to do is subtract 5. That will tell you what the dice originally read.

Suppose he throws a 4 and a 3.

He writes down 4.

He multiplies by 2, and adds 1: he gets 9.

He multiplies by 5: he gets 45.

He adds the 3 from the other die: he gets 48.

He tells you 48.

You subtract 5 and get 43.

51

The first digit 4 represents the first die; the 3, the other die.

You tell him he threw a 4 and a 3.

This will work beautifully for brothers and sisters, uncles and aunts, or sons and daughters instead of dice. Just substitute the number of brothers for the number on one die and the number of sisters for the number on the other die, and go by the same rule. For example:

1. Write down the number of brothers you have.
2. Double it and add 1.
3. Multiply by 5.
4. Add the number of sisters.
5. Tell the result.

You deduct 5 from this and there are your brothers and sisters next to one another.

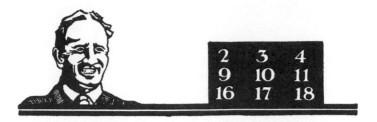

THREE IN SEQUENCE

Write down any three consecutive numbers (no number to be greater than 50), and add them together.

Now add any multiple of 3 you wish—but *tell* *me* the number you are adding.

Multiply this result by 67.

Tell me the last two digits in your answer, and I'll tell you the original three numbers you chose, as well as your complete answer.

Drawing the curtain aside:

Suppose you write down: 8, 9 and 10.

```
1. Adding them, you get a total of..........    27
2. Now add a multiple of 3, say 15...........   15
                                               ----
                                                42
3. Now multiply your result by 67............   67
                                               ----
                                               294
                                               252
                                               ----
                                               2814
4. Ask for the last 2 digits................    14
```

Before you ask for the last two figures, divide the multiple of 3 which was added (in this case it was 15) by 3. This gives you 5. Add 1 to 5 and you get 6.

As soon as you hear the last two digits, subtract this 6 from them. This tells you the *first* of the three numbers chosen originally. His three numbers, therefore, will be 8, 9 and 10. To get the entire result, you just multiply his last two digits by 2. This will tell you the first two digits of his answer.

In working this trick in a parlor, it's best to add a touch of showmanship. Ask your guest to write down any three consecutive numbers (no single number greater than 50), and add them together. Now ask any one in the room to give you any number under 40 which is divisible by 3. (As soon as you hear this number, you mentally divide it by 3 and add one to the result—this is your "key" number and you must remember it.)

Tell your guests to add that number to the sum of the three consecutive numbers.

Now tell them to multiply the result by 67. But here's how to do it:

Instead of asking your guest to multiply by 67 right off the bat, ask him to multiply his result by either 6 or 7. Now pause, and then say, "Better yet, make it 67!" If this is done neatly, the effect will be one of complete indifference to the importance of 67.

Now ask your hapless prey for the last two digits of his result, and then subtract your key number from it. In each case you will get the first of the three consecutive numbers he chose. And again, to get the final result, you merely multiply the last two digits he gives you by 2, and the first two are yours.

Let's take one more example to make sure you understand. Take 16, 17 and 18.

1. Adding these we get 51.
2. Now call for a multiple of 3. Suppose 21 is suggested. Adding 21 to 51 we get 72.
   (In the meantime divide 21 by 3 and add 1. 8 is therefore your key number.)

3. Multiply 72 by 67:

$$\begin{array}{r} 72 \\ 67 \\ \hline 504 \\ 432 \\ \hline 4824 \end{array}$$

When you hear 24 (the last two digits), deduct your key number, 8, and you have 16, 17 and 18, the three consecutive numbers. Double this 24, and you have 48, or the first two numbers of the final answer.

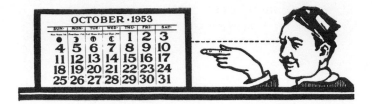

BIRTHDATE TRICK

You don't have to tell me—*I'll tell you* the exact date of your birth. Just do as I say.

1. Put down the number of the month in which you were born, taking January as month No. 1.
2. Add to this the next higher number in sequence.
3. Multiply by 5.
4. Add a zero to the right of your total.
5. Add any number less than 100 to your result. Tell me the number you added.
6. Now add the day of the month in which you were born.
7. Write down any number less than 100, tell it to me, and place this to the right of your result.
8. Add the last two numerals of the year of your birth.
9. Tell me your total and I will tell you your birthday—year, month and day.

Here is how it is done:

Suppose your friend was born February 12, 1899. According to schedule, he does the following:

1. Puts down the month.................... 2
2. Adds the next higher number............ 3
   _____
   5
3. Multiplies by 5........................ 25
4. Adds a zero to the right............... 250
5. Adds any number under 100 (let us say 32)
   —he tells you this number before he adds it
   to 250 282
6. Adds the day of the month.............. 12
   _____
   294
7. He takes another number under 100, tells it
   to you, and places it at the right. Thus, if he
   takes 22 29422
8. He adds the last two figures of his birth year
   and tells you the result................. 99
   _____
   29521

While your quivering kill is doing all this, you can quietly prepare yourself as follows:

1. Add 50 to the first number he told you in
   step 5 32
                                          50
                                          _____
                                          82
2. Add the second number he told you in step 7
   to the right of 82, thus................ 8222
3. Now, subtract this 8222 from the final total
   he gives you, thus:
   His result 29521
   Deduct 8222
                        _____
                        21299
4. Now mark off 2/12/99 and you get February 12, 1899.

HOW TO MAKE MILLIONS

Suppose a multimillionaire showed you his bank deposits over a period of 8 days, exactly as shown below, and told you that if you added the entire 6 columns correctly in less than 8 seconds, he would willingly give you a sum of money equal to the result— would you be a millionaire, or would you just be yourself?

$$264321$$
$$725463$$
$$542564$$
$$535235$$
$$735679$$
$$274537$$
$$457436$$
$$432413$$

If you knew this trick, you would win all the money the millionaire so freely promised.

Examining the columns shown above, you will see that the sum of the 1st and 5th rows is 1,000,000. This is also true for the sum of the 2nd and 6th rows, and for the sum of the 3rd and 7th rows. The total sum of these 6 rows, therefore, is 3,000,000.

Now let's eliminate these 6 rows, and you'll have only the 4th and 8th remaining. Note that in the 4th row, there is no number greater than 5, and in the 8th row, there is no number greater than 4. All you need do, therefore, is add the 4th and 8th rows and place a 3 to the left of the result to get the answer.

Simple?

1. In working this trick, tell your subject to write down, one beneath the other, three six-figure numbers.

2. When this is done, ask him to write below it another six-figure number with no figure greater than 5 in it.

3. Beneath his four numbers, you must now quickly write three additional six-figure numbers. Each number that you write, however, must, when added to one of your friend's numbers, total 1,000,000. For example:

   Suppose one of his numbers is 629701. Your corresponding number, therefore, must be 370299. (The easiest way to find the corresponding number needed to make up the 1,000,000, is to subtract each figure in the subject's number from 9 except the last which should be subtracted from 10. Always start from the left.)

4. Once you have found your three numbers, ask your subject to write down one more six-figure number with no digit greater than 4.

5. When he has done this, draw a line beneath all eight numbers, write down the 3 at the extreme left, and then start adding rows 4 and 8 from left to right. This will take you but a few seconds.

Here's a snapshot of the trick in action:

755279 ⎞
416935 ⎬ *these are what your friend*
804672 ⎠ *wrote*

A. (no digit greater than 5) : 542332 ⎞
244721 ⎬ these are what you write
583065 ⎠ to "neutralize" the three
195328   he wrote

B. (no digit greater than 4) : 343102   *he wrote this*

———————

3885434 ⎛ You merely write down a
⎜ 3 at the extreme left and
⎜ add A and B from left to
⎝ right.

MULTIPRACTICE

Here's another cute one to practice on a friend:

1. Ask him to write down the following number: twelve million, three hundred and forty-five thousand, six hundred and seventy-nine (12,345,679). (Note that the number eight is omitted.)

2. Now ask your friend which number of all these he likes the least, and when he gives you his answer, tell him to place an "x" above the number he selected.

3. At this point, instruct him to multiply the original 12,345,-679 by a number which you suggest.

4. Once he multiplies as directed, he will find that every figure in his total corresponds to the number above which he put the "x."

Example:

$$
\begin{array}{r}
\overset{\text{x}}{12,345,679} \\
45 \\
\hline
61,728,395 \\
493,827,16 \\
\hline
555,555,555
\end{array}
$$

61

Explanation:

It really doesn't matter what number your friend selects. Merely multiply that number by 9. Thus, in the case shown above, you multiply 5×9 and get 45. Once you have this total, multiply 12,345,679 by it.

The number 12,345,679 has some interesting features, for example:

$$\left.\begin{array}{l} 12,345,679 \times 3 = 037,037,037 \\ 12,345,679 \times 30 = 370,370,370 \\ 12,345,679 \times 57 = 703,703,703 \end{array}\right\} \text{Totals } 30$$

$$\left.\begin{array}{l} 12,345,679 \times 6 = 074,074,074 \\ 12,345,679 \times 33 = 407,407,407 \\ 12,345,679 \times 60 = 740,740,740 \end{array}\right\} \text{Totals } 33$$

$$\left.\begin{array}{l} 12,345,679 \times 12 = 148,148,148 \\ 12,345,679 \times 39 = 481,481,481 \\ 12,345,679 \times 66 = 814,814,814 \end{array}\right\} \text{Totals } 39$$

$$\left.\begin{array}{l} 12,345,679 \times 15 = 185,185,185 \\ 12,345,679 \times 42 = 518,518,518 \\ 12,345,679 \times 69 = 851,851,851 \end{array}\right\} \text{Totals } 42$$

$$\left.\begin{array}{l} 12,345,679 \times 21 = 259,259,259 \\ 12,345,679 \times 48 = 592,592,592 \\ 12,345,679 \times 75 = 925,925,925 \end{array}\right\} \text{Totals } 48$$

$$\left.\begin{array}{l} 12,345,679 \times 24 = 296,296,296 \\ 12,345,679 \times 51 = 629,629,629 \\ 12,345,679 \times 78 = 962,962,962 \end{array}\right\} \text{Totals } 51$$

Note: The middle multiple in each group equals the sum of the digits of any one result in that group.

The sum of all multiples in brackets equals the sum of all the digits of the results either across or up and down in that group.

For example: 33 in the second group equals the sum of all the digits in any 9 digit number in that group, as 407,407,407. The sum of *all* the 27 digits in this group equals the sum of the 3 multipliers, *i. e.,* the sum of 6, 33 and 60.

TOPSY TURVY

Here's one with an O. Henry ending.

Ask two of your friends, preferably a man and a girl, to assist you.

Have them place two chairs back to back.

Ask each to take one of the chairs, and inform the girl that her name henceforth is to be Topsy, and that the man's name is to be Turvy.

Obviously one can't see what the other is doing, since they are sitting back to back.

Now instruct them as follows:

"Agree between yourselves to select three numbers unknown to me. The first of these numbers must be between 10 and 45. The difference between the first and the second must be the same as the difference between the second and the third."

"Now, will each of you kindly add the three numbers together."

To Topsy: "Multiply your result by 3 or 4—better make it 34."*

---

* The reason for saying "3 or 4—better make it 34" is merely to throw your audience off the track, since someone might observe that 34 is approximately ⅓ of 100 and 67 is approximately ⅔ of 100 and might go on from there to discover the trick.

To Turvy: "Multiply your result by 67."

Then say: "I am going to ask you both a question. Don't answer until I count three, then both answer together. Ready, Topsy, what are the *first* two digits in your answer? Turvy, what are the *last* two digits in your answer?

"1—2—3." (At this point, both Topsy and Turvy will answer with the same digits.)

After you have done this, you can reverse the process and ask Turvy for his first two digits and Topsy for her last two digits, counting three again before they are to answer, and they will both reply with the same digits. This will turn out to be twice as large as the number previously named.

Example:

Suppose the three numbers written by Topsy and Turvy, unknown to you, were 24, 28 and 32. They each add these three and of course get 84.

Now you told Topsy to multiply her result by 34. She gets 2856.

You then tell Turvy to multiply his result by 67. He gets 5628. The result is obvious.

This rule applies to any three numbers that Topsy and Turvy may select between 10 and 45, which fulfill the requirements originally laid down.

THINK OF A CARD

Here's what the world's been waiting for—a cardless card trick. All you need do is ask someone to think of any card in the deck, giving the value of 11 to a Jack, 12 to a Queen, 13 to a King and 1 to an Ace. Now you will guarantee in only one quick trick to tell him what card he is thinking of.

Here's the technique:

1. Think of a card.
2. Now add the number of the card next higher in sequence. (If he s thinking of a King, add 14.)
3. Multiply the result by 5.
4. Now recall to him the old auction bridge value of the suits: Clubs, 6—Diamonds, 7—Hearts, 8—Spades, 9 and tell him to add the value of the suit to his total.
5. Ask for his result.
6. Mentally deduct 5, and tell him the card he thought of.

Example:

Suppose he thinks of the 9 of Diamonds   9

   1. He adds the next card higher in sequence   10
                                                                    19
   2. Multiply by 5   5
                                                                  95
   3. Add the suit value (Diamonds = 7)   7
                                                              102
   4. As soon as you hear 102, subtract 5   5

     And you get 97.

The first figure tells you the card he was thinking of. The second figure shows you the suit it was in.

AN AMAZING MEMORY TRICK

With this trick at your command, you can get a reputation for a memory as good as Macauley's. Your reputation will be thoroughly undeserved.

In the table below, you will see 49 key numbers with circles around them. Under each key number there is a number of seven figures.

Ask anyone to select a number in the circle, and offer to tell him the seven-figure number beneath it.

You must admit that this will be quite a substantial memory stunt —that is, if it involved any memory at all.

But here is how it's done:

1. Add 11 to the number selected.
2. Reverse the result.
3. Keep on adding the two previous numbers, leaving out the 10's.

Example:

Suppose the victim chooses 32.

1. You add 11 and get 43.
2. Reverse this 43 and you have the first two figures in your final answer, viz. 34.

3. Add the 3 and 4 and you get 7.
4. Add the 7 and 4 and get 11. (Omit 10—just put down the 1.)
5. The next figure is the 1 plus the 7, which is 8.
6. The next figure is the 8 plus 1 which is 9.
7. The next figure is the 9 plus 8, which is 17. (Just put down 7.)

This naturally produces the number.

You can make up a table of your own, using this principle and carrying out the numbers to as many places as you wish. Remember: The more credit you get for your remarkable memory, the less you deserve.

(23)	(39)	(18)	(22)	(4)	(38)	(16)
4370774	0550550	9213471	3369549	5167303	9437077	7291011
(2)	(45)	(30)	(34)	(25)	(6)	(15)
3145943	6516730	1459437	5493257	6392134	7189763	6280886
(9)	(37)	(46)	(3)	(1)	(17)	(32)
0224606	8426842	7527965	4156178	2134718	8202246	3471897
(21)	(5)	(44)	(11)	(41)	(19)	(8)
2358314	6178538	5505505	2246066	2572910	0336954	9101123
(29)	(12)	(33)	(13)	(43)	(7)	(10)
0448202	3257291	4482022	4268426	4594370	8190998	1235831
(49)	(14)	(24)	(47)	(26)	(40)	(28)
0662808	5279651	5381909	8538190	7303369	1561785	9325729
(31)	(27)	(35)	(48)	(20)	(42)	(36)
2460662	8314594	6404482	9549325	1347189	3583145	7415617

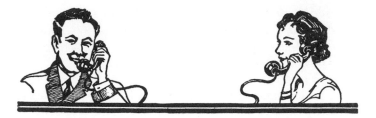

TELE-PHONEY

This is really two tricks in one. Once you have mastered the first, you will be able to do the second over the telephone if the mood strikes you.

Like most mathemagical stunts, this one appears complicated, but is really quite simple. All you need do is pay close attention to the directions. You will master the routine in no time.

A

Tell the quarry to write down any digit from 1 to 9, inclusive. Then direct him as follows:

1. Affix a cipher to the right of the digit he wrote down.
2. Add the original digit.
3. Multiply the result by 3.
4. Multiply this result by 11.
5. Multiply the final result by 3.
6. Then ask him to tell you the *last digit* of his answer.

You can then tell him his complete answer. It is all very simple. The answer is always in four digits.

When he tells you the last digit of his answer, all you need do is subtract it from 9, and you have the second digit of his answer.

The *first* digit will always be *one more* than the *second* digit.

The *third* digit will be the *first digit subtracted from nine.*

For example:

Suppose he tells you his last digit is 4. You will then instantly know that the second digit is 5, the first digit is 6, and the third digit is 3. Hence the entire number must be 6,534.

The table below will give you all the possible numbers from 1 to 9 that can be taken. It might be a good idea to study this table in order to understand the trick more fully. Note that the first digit is always the same as the digit your friend originally selected.

1st	2nd	3rd	4th
1	0	8	9
2	1	7	8
3	2	6	7
4	3	5	6
5	4	4	5
6	5	3	4
7	6	2	3
8	7	1	2
9	8	0	1

You will note, of course, that the basis of this trick is the number 1089. Each number that your friend takes originally is sure to be a factor of 1089.

B

Now let's consider part two of this stunt.

Before you call up your friend, consult your local telephone book (it must have at least 980 pages). Look up the ninth name on page 108, the eighth name on page 217, the seventh name on page 326, etc. Write these names down with addresses and telephone numbers in their respective places on your copy of the table on next page.

You are now ready to telephone your friend. When he answers, tell him to take a number from 1 to 9, inclusive, and then give the directions as explained in part A.

When he tells you the last digit of his result, ask him if he knows so-and-so (looking at your list) whose address is so-and-so and whose telephone number is so-and-so. No, he has never heard of him. Tell him then, to make a note of the name and telephone number which you give him.

Now tell him to look on the page in the telephone book corresponding to the first three digits of his answer and count down to the name represented by the fourth digit. By this time he has forgotten he ever gave you the last digit and of course he cannot imagine how you ever did it. Ask him what he finds.

The beauty of this trick is that you can repeat it, asking him to take another number to try it again. It is child's play, for you have in front of you the complete table with all the names.

Copy down on a piece of paper the table shown below (here you will note that instead of 1089, the number is 108-9, etc.). Look up the corresponding names with their 'phone numbers in a telephone book and you will be ready to try this trick out on your friends.

Page	Name	Telephone No.
108—9	B. C. Adams	———
217—8	C. B. Allen	———
326—7	E. Homer	———
435—6	C. Larsen	———
544—5	R. C. Miles	———
653—4	F. E. Powell	———
762—3	S. L. Quinby	———
871—2	E. P. Ransome	———
980—1	C. C. Slayton	———

AT A GLANCE

Here is the way to sum up as many numbers as you like at one single glance:

Example: The sum of all odd numbers up to and including 27?

Answer: 196—just like that!

Example: The sum of *all* numbers up to and including 27?

Answer: 378—just as quickly.

It's quite elementary. Here's how it's done.

All you have to do in the case of odd numbers, is add 1 to the final number in the series, divide by 2, and multiply the result by itself.

Example:

1. Find the sum of all odd numbers up to and including 19:

$$\begin{aligned}
\text{Add 1 to 19} &= 20 \\
\text{Divide by 2} &= 10 \\
\text{Square 10} &= 100
\end{aligned}$$

Answer is 100

72

2. The sum of all odd numbers up to and including 49:

> Add 1 to 49 =   50
> Divide by 2 =   25
> Square 25   = 625

> Answer is 625

To find the sum of *all* numbers, odd and even, up to and including a given odd number, proceed as before, double the square, and subtract the square root, thus:

1. To find the sum of *all* numbers up to and including 17:

> Add 1 to 17 =   18
> Divide by 2 =   9
> Square 9   =   81   (Sum of odd numbers)
> Double this = 162
> Subtract 9   = 153

> Answer is 153

2. The sum of all numbers from 1 to 29, inclusive:

> Add 1 to 29 =   30
> Divide by 2 =   15
> Square 15   = 225   (Sum of odd numbers)
> Double this = 450
> Subtract 15 = 435

> Answer is 435

PSYCHIC BRIDGE

Here's a new way to discover just how many points your friend won or lost at Contract bridge, without being in the game with him.

1. Tell him to write down the number of points he won or lost in one session, and put a circle around the last two digits.
2. Now tell him to multiply the figure or figures which are not in the circle by 2, and add 1 to the result.
3. Now multiply this total by 5.
4. Add to this the first figure in the circle (if the number in the circle were 10, he would add 1).
5. Place a zero to the right of the result.
6. Now tell him: "If you won in your last game, that is *odd* —so add either 111, 113, 117 or 119 to your total. If you lost (*even* you might) add 112, 114, 116 or 118. Don't tell me what number you are adding."
7. Ask him to *tell* you how many rubbers were played, to add that number to his result, and then to tell you his final answer.

Upon hearing this answer, you will be able to tell him exactly how many points he won or lost.

Here's how to become a psychic bridge expert:

1. Deduct the number of rubbers played from the final result given you.

2. If the last figure is *even*, he *lost;* if it is *odd*, he *won*. This last figure tells you, incidentally, what number he added at step 6. If it is a 1, he added 111; if it is a 2, he added 112; if it is a 3, he added 113, etc.

3. Now all you need do is to subtract that number, plus the number of rubbers played, plus 50, from the answer he originally gave you. This tells you the number of points he won or lost.

Let's suppose your friend is a rather poor contract player. In one hand he was set 2,000 points. He trumped his partner's Aces a number of times that evening and kept bidding small slams on bust hands. The net result of all this rather unusual bridge playing was a maximum set-back for the evening of 11,630 points in three rubbers.

Now eliminating his wife or his partner as a factor contributing to this debacle, let's consider just what this poor dupe does when he follows your instructions.

What You Say	**What He Does**
1. Put down the number of points you won or lost and encircle the last two digits.	He puts down 11630, and encircles the last two digits 11630
2. Double the digits that are not in the circle and add 1 to the result.	He multiplies 116 by 2. 232 He adds 1 .... 1 ——— 233
3. Multiply by 5.	He multiplies by 5.... 5 ——— 1165
4. Add the first of the two digits in the circle.	He adds 3 .... 3 ——— 1168
5. Place a cipher to the right of your result.	He places a zero to the right of 1168 which gives him 11680
6. If you won, "that's *odd*," so add either 111, 113, 117 or 119. If you lost ("*even* you might"), add 112, 114, 116 or 118.	He knows he lost. He adds one of the four even numbers last mentioned. Let's suppose he chooses 116 .... 116 He gets 11796
7. Tell me how many rubbers you played; add that to your present total and tell me your answer.	He tells you he played three rubbers. He adds this to 11796 .... 3 ——— 11799

When you hear the number 11,799, the first thing to do is to subtract 3 (the number of rubbers played). This gives you 11796. The last digit of this number is always the same as the last digit of the number he added in step 6. The 6 at the end of this number, therefore, immediately tells you that your friend added 116 and since this number is even, he must have lost.

All you do now is add 116, 3, and 50. This gives you 169.*

Subtract this 169 from the number he told you, which was 11799. The result is 11,630 points lost.

Upon achieving this result, it is best to make no comment regarding your friend's bridge playing.

---

* The 116 is the number your friend added. The 3 is the number of rubbers played and the 50 is your key number.

JUGGLING THE TIME

The next time you miss the 5:17 and have to wait for the 5:43, sit down in the station in front of a clock, take out a piece of paper and a pencil and try this trick on yourself.

Draw a circle and divide it into 12 equal parts, as shown below.

Start where one o'clock would be and put the multiples of 3 all around the clock.

When you have done this, start again at one o'clock and put the multiples of 4 next to the multiples of 3 as indicated.

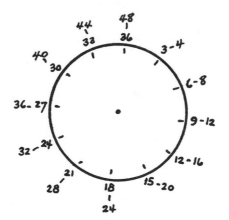

Now you have put in the numbers indicated, and you will discover these following startling facts.

If you subtract the smaller number from the larger number in each case you will get the hour, which you can now place on the clock.

If you subtract the smaller number from the larger number and add the result to the larger number, you will get the number of minutes.

If you square each of these two numbers and add them together, you will find that the result in every case equals the square of the minutes they represent. Some say that this is how Times Square got its name.

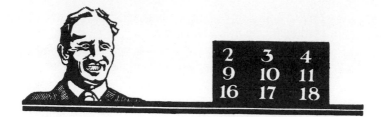

ALWAYS THE SAME NUMBER

I'm sorry—it's quite hopeless—your answer will always be 109989 no matter what five-digit number you take.* You don't believe it? All right:

On a blank page write *any* five-digit number. Now rewrite this number with the first and last digits interchanged.

Subtract the smaller number from the greater one, and write the result on another part of the paper.

Rewrite this number, with the first and last digit interchanged, directly under it.

This time, *add* the two numbers and your answer is 109989!

Here it is, worked out for you:

1. Suppose you wrote down... 47631
2. And under it............. 17634   (1st and last figure
   Subtract 29997   reversed)
3. Now you write this result............. 29997
4. Then you rewrite it, reversing the extremes
   (as before) 79992
   And add 109989

---

* With this exception the difference between the first and last digits of the number selected must, however, be greater than unity.

Try one of your own and convince yourself.

If you had taken a six-digit number instead of a five-digit number, the answer would have been 1099989. If you had taken a seven-digit number, the answer would have been 10999989.

The secret is this: The first two digits are always 1-0. The last two are always 8-9, regardless of how many digits (above 4) are in your original number. The number of 9's separating the first two digits from the last two digits is always 3 less than the number of digits in your original number. Thus:

> If your original number has 4 digits the number is   10989
> If your original number has 5 digits the number is   109989
> If your original number has 6 digits the number is 1099989
> If your original number has 7 digits the number is 10999989
>
>   etc.

In working this trick, be sure that your friend tells you how many digits there are in the number he takes. If you want to take a chance and watch your friend's pencil as he writes his number, you may be able to see for yourself how many digits he wrote down, even if you can't tell what the number was.

A DETECTRICK

Here's a good after-dinner trick calculated to mess up the table-cloth in no uncertain fashion. You need only the following equipment: 24 matches, a knife, a fork and a spoon. If the knife, fork and spoon are not handy, you might use a salt cellar, a pepper shaker and a napkin.

Now corral three assistants. Let's call them Mr. 1, Mr. 2 and Mr. 3.

Give Mr. 1 one match.

Give Mr. 2 two matches.

Give Mr. 3 three matches.

Now place the knife, the fork and the spoon in front of you.

Place on the center of the table the remaining eighteen matches.

Turn your back and instruct your assistants as follows: "While I am not looking, I want one of you to take up the knife; another the fork; and the third, the spoon. Put these objects in your pockets where they can't be seen.

"Now I want the person who has the knife to take as many matches from the center of the table as I originally gave him.

"I want the one who chose the fork to take twice as many matches from the center of the table as I originally gave him.

"Whoever has the spoon must take four times as many as I originally gave him.

"Each one of you must now conceal his own matches so that I can't see them."

At this point, turn around and tell your bewildered audience *which article each one chose.*

If you stop to figure the possibilities, you will find that of the eighteen original matches on the table there can only be the following amounts left: 1, 2, 3, 5, 6 or 7. These six numbers are paired off into three groups as follows: 1 and 3; 2 and 6; 5 and 7.

And here are the only possible distributions:

		Knife	*Fork*	*Spoon*
Group 1:	1	Mr. 1 has	Mr. 2 has	Mr. 3 has
	3	Mr. 1 has	Mr. 3 has	Mr. 2 has
Group 2:	2	Mr. 2 has	Mr. 1 has	Mr. 3 has
	6	Mr. 2 has	Mr. 3 has	Mr. 1 has
Group 3:	5	Mr. 3 has	Mr. 1 has	Mr. 2 has
	7	Mr. 3 has	Mr. 2 has	Mr. 1 has

For example: If there are six matches left on the table, you know instantly this falls into group 2, where Mr. 2 has the knife, Mr. 3 has the fork and Mr. 1 has the spoon. You will note that the *knife* group always has the *group* number. If it is in group 1, Mr. 1 has the knife; if it is in group 2, Mr. 2 has the knife; if it is in group 3, Mr. 3 has the knife.

Note, also, that the larger number of the two in the group indicates that the larger number person has the fork.

For example: Suppose there are seven matches left on the table. Instantly you know that 7 is the larger of the two numbers in group 3, so that Mr. 3 must have the knife (the knife group always has the group number). Since the larger number in the group indicates that the larger number person has the fork, Mr. 2 must have the fork and Mr. 1 the spoon. If there are only two matches, you know that this is in group 2, so that Mr. 2 must have the knife, Mr. 1 must have the fork (since 2 is the *smaller* number in group 2), and Mr. 3 must have the spoon.

DIGITSLIPS

For a change, we have one that has no connection with arithmetic or geometry or mathemagic or the like. It merely goes to prove how silly our reactions are at times.

1. Corner your quarry.
2. Now tell him that you are going to give him ten numbers *very quickly.*
3. After each number he must say the next higher one. (If you say 10, he must say 11, etc.)
4. Tell him that you are going to go very fast, and offer to bet him anything he likes he won't get every number correct.

Here's the list:

$$66$$
$$12$$
$$123$$
$$7$$
$$149$$
$$315$$
$$212$$
$$1196$$
$$78$$
$$4099$$

Nine out of ten people will say 5,000 after the last number.

FIGURE THIS OUT

When a child reaches $\frac{1}{11}$ the age of its mother when the child is born, the mother will be 12 times the age of the child. For example: If the child is 2 and the mother is 24, the mother is 12 times the age of the child, yet a child of 2 is $\frac{1}{11}$ of its mother's age when it was born. (Its mother was then 22.)

When a child reaches $\frac{1}{10}$ of the age of its mother when it was born, the mother will then be 11 times the age of the child—and for the same reason.

Similarly:

When the child reaches $\frac{1}{9}$ of its mother's age when it was born, the mother will be 10 times the age of the child.

When the child reaches $\frac{1}{8}$ of its mother's age when it was born, the mother will be 9 times the age of the child.

When the child reaches $\frac{1}{2}$ of its mother's age when it was born, the mother will be three times the age of the child.

When the child reaches the same age its mother was when it was born, the mother will be twice the age of the child.

When will the child reach its mother's age?

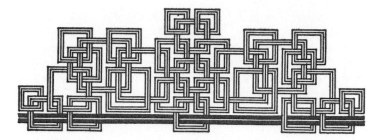

MAGIC SQUARES

Magic squares were known to the ancients and were thought to possess mystic and magical powers because of their unusual nature. Astronomers of old tried vainly to find relations between magic squares and the planets, and in India even at the present time magic squares are worn engraven on stone or metal as talismans. For centuries these wonderful arrangements of numbers have fascinated all who have the slightest interest in mathematics.

There are hundreds of different methods of forming magic squares but only the easiest and most intelligible have been given here.

The simplest magic square has 3 cells on a side, or 9 cells altogether as shown in figure A. Let us call this a three square.

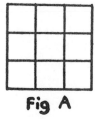

Fig A

8	1	6
3	5	7
4	9	2

Fig B

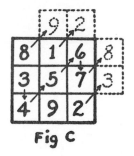

Fig C

It is necessary, in order to make this into a magic square, to place a different number (from 1 to 9 inclusive) in each cell in such a way that the sum of every horizontal row of cells, the sum of every vertical column of cells, and the sum of the two diagonals, shall add up to the same number. This is done for you in figure B, where you can readily see that the sum of each horizontal row equals 15, the sum of each vertical column equals 15, and the two diagonals each adds up to 15.

The numbers are always placed consecutively in the square moving in a right oblique direction (indicated by the arrows) in figure C.

Always start by placing number 1 in the middle cell of the top row. Now go right oblique upward and you will note that the next number which is 2 comes *above* and outside this square in the dotted cell. In this case drop the 2 to the *lowest* cell in that column. Now go right oblique upwards again and you find the next number, 3, comes outside of the square to the *right*. In this case move the 3 to the extreme *left* cell in that row. Now you will note that the number 1 interferes with the next right oblique upward move, therefore drop down one cell and place the 4 directly below the 3. Now you have clear sailing for 5 and 6. It is impossible to go right oblique from this corner (since there is no cell corresponding to this move) hence, drop down in the square as before, placing the 7 directly below the 6, and continue as before, placing the 8 and 9 in their proper locations as shown in figure C.

Practice this 9-cell magic square by yourself—without the dotted lines as guides. When you have mastered this start with any number instead of the number 1. Remember whatever number you start with must always be placed in the middle cell of the top row.

When you have worked out a few magic squares of 9 cells try the next odd square—the 5 square which has 25 cells. Exactly the same principle is applied to this 5 square, as a study of figure D will reveal. You will note that the first number is in the center of the top row and the direction (indicated by the arrows) is always right oblique. With a little practice you ought to be able to make a 5-cell magic square. The same principle applies to any magic square with an uneven number of cells. If you have no difficulty in constructing the 5 square correctly you will have no difficulty in constructing the 7 square, the 9 square and all other odd number magic squares.

We saw that in the 3 square all the rows and columns added up to 15. What will they add up to in the 5 square, the 7 square, the 9 square, or any other square? Here is the general rule which applies for odd and even cell magic squares which start with the number 1. If you know the number of cells on a side you can instantly arrive at the sum of all the rows, columns, and diagonals, merely by:

1. Cubing the number of cells in a row.
2. Adding the number of cells in a row to the result.
3. Dividing the result by 2.

For example, a 5-cell magic square would have rows and columns adding up to 65, because, according to the above rule, 5 cubed plus 5, divided by 2, equals 65. A 6-cell magic square would have rows and columns adding up to 111, because 6 cubed plus 6, divided by 2, equals 111.

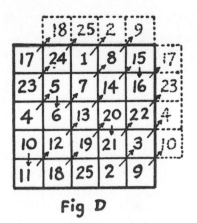

Fig D

The even-cell magic squares are formed entirely differently from the odd-cell magic squares. Let us take a 4-cell square and examine the way to construct it. The first thing to do is to draw 2 diagonals (figure E). In the upper left-hand corner start with number 1 but do not put it in because it is on the diagonal. Now, running directly across, place 2 and 3 in the next two cells but omit 4 from the fourth cell, since this is also on the diagonal. Continue this right along consecutively as shown in figure E, putting in numbers where there is *no* diagonal and omitting the numbers where there *is* a diagonal. When you have done this you will have figure E.

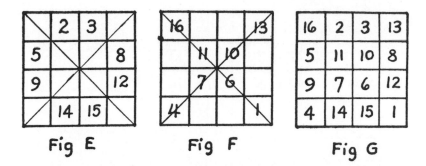

Fig E   Fig F   Fig G

Now start with number 16 (the highest number which was omitted in figure E because it was on the diagonal) in the upper left-hand corner cell of figure F. Now count backwards from 16 for each cell, so that when you come to the next cell which is crossed by a diagonal (the last cell in the top row) your number will be 13. Continue this, writing down these numbers in every cell crossed by the diagonal as shown in figure F. When you have done this your final result will be the magic square shown in figure G. This is a 4 square which according to the rule should have diagonals, rows and columns which add up to 34 (4 cubed plus 4 divided by 2).*

The 8 square—the magic square with eight cells on a side—is constructed on the same principle. Merely draw the two main diagonals and divide the square into four 4-cell squares as indicated by the heavy lines. Now draw the other diagonals as shown in figure H. The same principle applies here as did in the 4 square. You start with number 1 in the upper left-hand cell, omitting it because it is on the diagonal. Continue right along consecutively putting in all the numbers not on diagonals and omitting all numbers which are. You then have figure H. Now go back and, start-

---

* Note that the upper left 4 cells (16 + 2 + 5 + 11) = 34; the upper right 4 cells (3 + 13 + 10 + 8) = 34 as well as the lower left and lower right 4 cells = 34.

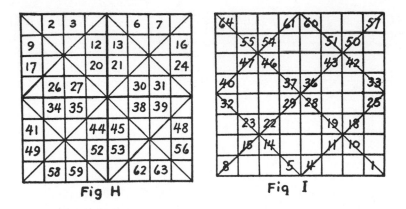

Fig H   Fig I

ing with the highest number (which is 64), you do exactly the reverse (figure I). Count backwards from 64, putting in the numbers only where the diagonal crosses the cell. When you are through you have a perfect 8 square which, according to our rule, has rows, columns, and diagonals adding up to 260 (figure J).

64	2	3	61	60	6	7	57
9	55	54	12	13	51	50	16
17	47	46	20	21	43	42	24
40	26	27	37	36	30	31	33
32	34	35	29	28	38	39	25
41	23	22	44	45	19	18	48
49	15	14	52	53	11	10	56
8	58	59	5	4	62	63	1

Fig J

Any magic square the number of whose cells on a side is a multiple of 4 can be constructed on this principle.

Now let us take the most difficult magic square of all—the 6 square. This is generally considered the most complicated of all the magic squares to construct. Here is the easiest method yet discovered.

The first thing to do is divide the 6 square into four 3 squares as indicated by the heavy lines in figure K. Start in the upper left-

8	1	6	26	19	24
3	5	7	21	23	25
4	9	2	22	27	20
35	28	33	17	10	15
30	32	34	12	14	16
31	36	29	13	18	11

Transpose (left side label)

Fig K

35	1	6	26	19	24
3	32	7	21	23	25
31	9	2	22	27	20
8	28	33	17	10	15
30	5	34	12	14	16
4	36	29	13	18	11

Fig L

hand 3 square and place the numbers from 1 to 9 in their proper cells exactly as you did in the regular 3 square. Next go to the lower right-hand 3 square and, starting with number 10, instead of 1, place your numbers from 10 to 18 exactly as you learned to do in the 3 square. Now go to the upper right-hand 3 square and, starting with number 19, place your numbers from 19 through 27 in the same way. Now finish in the lower left-hand 3 square, starting with 28 and ending with 36. Your square is now figure K and all you need to do to make it a perfect magic square of 6 is to transpose the three cells indicated by the zig-zag line—you merely place the 8, 5 and 4 where the 35, 32 and 31 are, and place the 35, 32 and 31 where the 8, 5 and 4 are. You then have figure L, a perfect magic square of 6 cells.

The methods given here are among the simplest. There are innumerable ways of constructing magic squares.

FUN WITH MAGIC SQUARES

Ask someone to give you any number of two digits. Suppose he gives you 24. You can now tell him that you will start with his number and build up a magic square of 4 cells on a side with every horizontal row, every perpendicular column and every diagonal adding up to 126. (You arrive at 126 by mentally multiplying the number he gave you by 4 and adding 30; if he had given you 16 instead of 24, the sum of the rows, columns and diagonals would be 94 instead of 126.) The next thing to do is to proceed to fill in the magic square of 4 just as you learned to do it, but instead of starting with number 1 you start with number 24. When you have finished you can show your friend a magic square starting with the number he gave you, all of whose rows, columns and diagonals add up to the number which you predicted they would add up to —126.

A simple rule to remember in this connection is the following: For a 3 square multiply the number given you by 3 and add 12. For a 4 square multiply the number given you by 4 and add 30. For a 5 square multiply the number given you by 5 and add 60. For a 7 square multiply the number given by 7 and add 168. It is not necessary to go any higher than this unless your friend is a perfect fool for magic squares.

Let's review this. Suppose you ask someone to give you a number in two digits and he gives you 34. Suppose you tell him you will construct a 7 square, starting with the number he gave you, all of whose rows, columns and diagonals shall add up to the same number. What is that number? According to rule it is $7 \times 34 + 168 = 406$. A slight amount of figuring will instantly give you this result and you can imagine your friend's astonishment when you have completed a very intricate-looking magic square with 7 cells on a side, all of whose rows, columns and diagonals add up to the number you predicted before you started.

TRANSPOSING MAGIC SQUARES

One of the most mystifying tricks that you can do with magic squares is to construct one whose rows, columns and diagonals all add up to any number your friend may give you (provided that number is greater than 15 for a 3 square, 34 for a 4 square, 65 for a 5 square, etc.). Before you can do this, however, it is necessary to learn the method of transposing.

Construct a magic square of 4 as you have already learned to do (see figure M). Now draw a blank 4 square (figure N) and

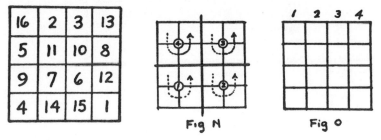

FIG. M

Fig N

Fig O

another blank 4 square (figure O). Divide N into 4 equal parts as indicated by the heavy lines. Each part has four cells. The lower left-hand group is called No. 1, the lower right group No. 2, the upper right group No. 3, and the upper left group No. 4. Now place a dotted U in each group as indicated. Next refer to figure M, which is the regular magic square of 4. By means of figure N you are going to transpose this regular magic square into the blank square, figure O.

Now start in by placing the numbers 1, 2, 3, 4 over the first, second, third, four columns in figure O as shown. Now commence in the lower left-hand group of figure M, referring to the dotted U-shaped line in figure N, transpose these four numbers in that order, namely, 9, 4, 14 and 7, into the first column of figure O. The 9 goes into the first column, the 4 underneath it, the 14 underneath

95

that and the 7 into the bottom cell. Now do the same thing for group 2, namely, take 6, 15, 1 and 12 and put them in column 2 of figure O in the same way.

Continue this procedure for group 3 and group 4, filling in column 3 and column 4 in figure O. The result will be the figure P. This figure P is the transposed magic square of figure M.

_1_	_2_	_3_	_4_
9	6	3	16
4	15	10	5
14	1	8	11
7	12	13	2

Fig P

17	24	1	8	15
23	5	7	14	16
4	6	13	20	22
10	12	19	21	3
11	18	25	2	9

Fig Q

The method of transforming the magic 5 square is slightly different. Consider the 5 square figure Q—this is a regular magic square of 25 cells. It is required to transform it into figure S.

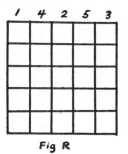

_1_	_4_	_2_	_5_	_3_

Fig R

_1_	_4_	_2_	_5_	_3_
23	6	19	2	15
4	12	25	8	16
10	18	1	14	22
11	24	7	20	3
17	5	13	21	9

Fig S

The first thing to do is to place above the first column of figure R, the number 1, skip a column, place No. 2 above the third column, skip a column and place No. 3 above the last column. Now go back and fill in No. 4 above the second column and No. 5 above the fourth column as shown.

The rest is very simple. Merely take the highest number in the first column of figure Q and put it in the cell represented by the number above the first column of figure R. Fill in the other four cells in this column in their proper order.

Now go to column 2 in figure Q, take the higher number in that column and place it in the cell indicated by the number above column 2 of figure R (the fourth cell down). Fill in the other numbers in rotation.

Continue this procedure for the next two columns and leave the last column alone. You then have a transformed magic square of 5 as shown in figure S.

A good way to apply this transformation and at the same time surprise your friends is to tell someone that you can construct a magic square which will add up to 34 in all directions. You then proceed to construct the regular 4 square. The next thing to do is to draw a blank magic square of 4 and proceed to fill it in from the first magic square by the method of transformation with which you are now familiar. (With a little practice you should be able to fill in any blank cell in the blank magic square which your friend may select, without going in order. Of course you always have the original magic square in front of you to guide you.) When you have completed the transposition, draw another blank magic 4 square. Now ask your friend to give you any number between 34 and 100. He selects 71. Tell him that you will construct a magic square which will add up to his number in all directions. Here is the way to do it:

1. Deduct 34 (the sum that the regular 4 square adds up to):
$$71 - 34 = 37$$

2. Divide the result by 4 (the number of cells on a side):
$37 \div 4 = 9$ and 1 over

3. Add 9 to every number in the transposed magic square except the four highest numbers (13, 14, 15 and 16). To these last four numbers you add both the 9 and the remaining 1, or 10.

Of course as you add each number mentally to the number in any cell in the transposed magic square, you promptly place it in the corresponding cell of your last blank magic square and you will find that every row, every column, and the two diagonals of this new magic square will add up to 71—the number your friend gave you.

If you want to do this with a 5 square, first construct a regular 5 square and a blank 5 square. Next make your transposition to fill this blank square. Now draw another blank 5 square and ask your friend for a number between 65 (the sum that the regular 5 square adds up to) and 100. He selects 93.

1. Deduct 65:
$$93 — 65 = 28$$

2. Divide by 5 (the number of cells on a side):
$$28 ÷ 5 = 5 \text{ and } 3 \text{ over}$$

3. Add 5 to every number in the transposed magic square except the five highest numbers (21, 22, 23, 24 and 25). To these last five numbers you add both the 5 and the remaining 3, or 8.

Proceed just as you did with the 4 square.

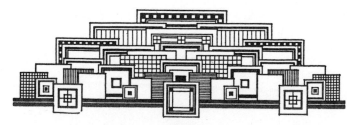

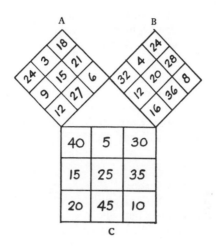

THE MAGIC TRIANGLE

The triangle in the diagram opposite is a right triangle. C is the square on the hypotenuse and A and B are the squares on the two equal sides.

If you examine it you will see that A, B and C are each magic squares. The square of any cell of C is equal to the sum of the squares of the corresponding cells in A and B. For example, 40^2 is equal to 24^2 plus 32^2.

Likewise the square of the sum of any two or more cells or any diagonal or horizontal row or any perpendicular column in C, is equal to the square of the sum of the corresponding two or more cells, rows, columns or diagonals of A plus B.

Also note that the square of the total of all the cells in C equals the square of the total of all the cells in A plus the square of the total of all the cells in B.

99

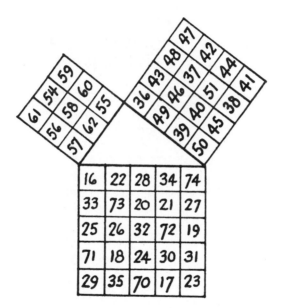

THE MAGIC SQUARE ON THE HYPOTENUSE OF A RIGHT TRIANGLE

Old Pythagoras made one error in his famous *pons asinorum:* He forgot that some day it would get into the hands of a magician. If he had mentioned that the *magic* square on the hypotenuse is equal to the sum of the *magic* squares of the other two sides he would have saved a lot of argument and this book would be two pages shorter.

Looking at these three magic squares you will note that the rows, columns and diagonals of each one of them adds up to 174; and *no two numbers are duplicated.*

The sum of all the numbers in the three square, squared, plus the sum of all the numbers in the four square, squared, equals the sum of all the numbers in the five square, squared.

THE MAGIC LOVERS

Each of these two romantic lovers forms a magic square of 66.

You will soon find out what happens when they embrace. But first let us consider them as you now see them.

Biologically speaking, the cells in the female tend to complement the cells in the male. For example: the four corner cells in Minnie (1, 31, 6 and 28, which total 66) complement the equivalent four corner cells in Otto (9, 23, 14 and 20, which total 66). This means that if you take away two of Minnie's corner cells, such as 1 and 28, Otto will come to the rescue, with his 9 and 20.

Furthermore, 4, 5, 31 and 26 of Minnie—forming a small square over the appendix—equals 12, 13, 23 and 18 of Otto in the same place. Now operate on Minnie, taking away the 4 and 31, and Otto, in order to keep Minnie's prognosis at 66, again comes to the rescue with his 12 and 23. Nice boy, Otto.

It may be briefly remarked that there are many other parts of their anatomies where this is possible.

We've held these lovers apart long enough. Let's promote a merger. Now they form a magic square of sexty-sex. Imagine the thrill of this loving embrace when Minnie's 1 and 31 come in contact with Otto's 20 and 14 to produce 66. This is only the beginning. . . .

On closer acquaintance it will be seen that Minnie's 8 and 26 coincide with Otto's 21 and 11, still forming the perfect union of 66. We leave it to you to discover other combinations forming 66, while they are in this position.

THE MAGIC GRIDIRON

The peculiar contrivance illustrated is a magic gridiron. Let us see what can be cooked up with it.

First you will notice that you can turn any one of the number-blocks around so that it is blank.

Notice that the gridiron is composed of nine major cells, with four blocks in each cell. The four-digit numbers in each cell are so arranged that they form a magic square totaling 16,335, horizontally, vertically and diagonally.

Now if you turn over the first three blocks in each cell, leaving only the fourth exposed, you will have a magic square totaling 15.

Now still leaving these nine blocks exposed as above, turn back the adjacent block to the left in each cell, so that the two right-hand blocks are visible. These will make a magic square totaling 135 in every direction.

Try this once more with three digits exposed in each cell, and you will discover again that you have made a magic square.

You have now found four different ways of turning around the blocks to make magic squares. There are 60 more arrangements possible with this gridiron. See if you can find them.

Here is a clue: in the upper left-hand corner, you see the number 8712. Suppose you turn the 2 around to the blank side, leaving 871. Now instead of 871 read this as 718. Make the corresponding change and reading for each of the other four-digit numbers in the rest of the cells. This will also form a magic square, won't it? There are only 59 more varieties for you to discover for yourself.

106

THE MAGIC EXPLOSION

The picture on the opposite page was taken in a number factory at the instant it blew up. It shows one peculiar thing about the explosion: its remarkable consistency, as you will find if you examine it.

For example: the difference between the square of any number and the square of the number diametrically opposite it is in all cases 2880.

The sum of the squares of any two numbers which are next to one another is equal to the sum of the squares of the numbers diametrically opposite these two. Note that:

$$184^2 - 176^2 = 2880$$
$$72^2 - 48^2 = 2880$$
$$63^2 - 33^2 = 2880$$
$$139^2 + 721^2 = 149^2 + 719^2$$
$$89^2 + 62^2 = 71^2 + 82^2$$
$$721^2 + 358^2 + 126^2 + 82^2 = 719^2 + 362^2 + 114^2 + 98^2$$

The more you study this remarkable explosion the more interesting facts you'll be able to find. The few given above are only the beginning.

58	12	24	38	63	13	17	35
3364	144	576	1444	3969	169	289	1225
53	7	27	41	52	2	30	48
2809	49	729	1681	2704	4	900	2304
14	64	36	18	11	57	37	23
196	4096	1296	324	121	3249	1369	529
1	51	47	29	8	54	42	28
1	2601	2209	841	64	2916	1764	784
40	22	10	60	33	19	15	61
1600	484	100	3600	1089	361	225	3721
43	25	5	55	46	32	4	50
1849	625	25	3025	2116	1024	16	2500
20	34	62	16	21	39	59	9
400	1156	3844	256	441	1521	3481	81
31	45	49	3	26	44	56	6
961	2025	2401	9	676	1936	3136	36
+	+	+	+	+	+	+	+

THE MAGIC SQUARE OF SQUARES

(See complementary square of squares on next page)

Nothing could be squarer than this. Not only do the white numbers in the black cells form a magic square totaling 260, but the numbers in black on the white squares also form a magic square totaling 11,180. The white numbers go from 1 to 64 inclusive. The black numbers in the white cells are their squares.

For example: take the first row of white numbers, namely, 58, 12, 24, 38, 63, 13, 17 and 35. You will note that the black number below each of these white numbers is its square.

46.4	9.6	19.2	30.4	50.4	10.4	13.6	28.
34.8	7.2	14.4	22.8	37.8	7.8	10.2	21.
42.4	5.6	21.6	32.8	41.6	1.6	24.	38.4
31.8	4.2	16.2	24.6	31.2	1.2	18.	28.8
11.2	51.2	28.8	14.4	8.8	45.6	29.6	18.4
8.4	38.4	21.6	10.8	6.6	34.2	22.2	13.8
0.8	40.8	37.6	23.2	6.4	43.2	33.6	22.4
0.6	30.6	28.2	17.4	4.8	32.4	25.2	16.8
32.	17.6	8.	48.	26.4	15.2	12.	48.8
24.	13.2	6.	36.	19.8	11.4	9.	36.6
34.4	20.	4.	44.	36.8	25.6	3.2	40.
25.8	15.	3.	33.	27.6	19.2	2.4	30.
16.	27.2	49.6	12.8	16.8	31.2	47.2	7.2
12.	20.4	37.2	9.6	12.6	23.4	35.4	5.4
24.8	36.	39.2	2.4	20.8	35.2	44.8	4.8
18.6	27.	29.4	1.8	15.6	26.4	33.6	3.6

THE COMPLEMENTARY MAGIC SQUARE
OF SQUARES

First consider the numbers in the upper part of each cell. They form a magic square. Now consider the numbers in the lower part of each cell. They also form a magic square.

Now subtract the lower number from the upper number in any cell and add this difference to the upper number. Your result will equal the white number in the corresponding black cell in the magic square of squares on the preceding page.

The sum of the squares of both numbers in any cell equals the black number in the corresponding white cell in the *magic square of squares*.

For example: in the second cell from the left on the top row we see 9.6 for the upper number and 7.2 for the lower. If you take the lower one from the upper your result will be 2.4 and if you add this to the upper your result will be 12. Referring to the corresponding cell in the magic square of squares on a preceding page we see the *white* number 12.

Now, squaring 9.6 and 7.2 and adding them together your result will be 144 which also equals the corresponding cell in the magic square of squares in a preceding page where the *black* number appears.

THE MAGIC HONEYCOMB

How doth the mathematical bee make its hive?

He combs out all the numbers from 1 to 216, without any duplicates, and arranges them in his hive as follows:

He forms six major hexagonal honeycombs, each containing six concentric hexagons. Then he buzzes from cell to cell depositing the numbers in such a way that they add up to 651 around each concentric hexagon, of which there are 36 in all.

This is not his only secret. To him the honey of numbers is so sweet that by so doing he also makes every radius total 651, in each hexagon.

Now that the hive is completed, he can fly from the top center cell of any hexagon (*i. e.*, 1, 7, 13, 19, 25 or 31), go to the right spirally, visiting the proper cell in each concentric hexagon in turn, until he reaches the center; and the sum of all the stopping-places will also be 651. For example: in the top hexagon, 1, 68, 75, 142, 149, 216.

If, however, he prefers to fly in a left-hand spiral, he can start at the cell to the left of the top center in any hexagon (*i. e.*, 211, 205, 199, 193, 187 or 181), go to the left spirally, visiting the proper cell in each concentric hexagon in turn, until he reaches the center; and the sum of all the stopping-places will again be 651. For example: (211, 146, 141, 76, 71, 6).

THE MAGIC WEB

What is the secret woven into the spider's web?

He has pushed the dew-drops along each pair of threads so that they form a very interesting pattern, with the numbers from 1 to 64 inclusive, and with no duplication.

This intelligent spider has arranged these dew-drops so that they will add up to 65, 130, 195 and 260, in ways known only to him.

Dust the cob-webs off your brain by trying to find how many combinations can be formed from each one of the four above totals.

116

THE MAGIC WHEEL

See whether you can steer your course around this one without going on the rocks.

You know that there are 360 degrees in a circle. The handles at the end of each spoke will help you to grasp this idea.

From every spoke-handle to the hub the sum of the numbers is 360; also, one-half the spoke adds up to 180. But this isn't all. The total of the 1st, 3rd, 5th and 7th number in each spoke is 180. Likewise, the sum of the 2nd, 4th, 6th and 8th in any spoke is 180.

Now let us revolve the magic wheel. From the hub to the rim there are eight concentric circles. The sum of the numbers around every concentric circle is 360. Furthermore, the sum of the two numbers in each segment is 90 (the number of degrees in a quarter-circle).

See whether you can steer a course spirally around this wheel, from the proper starting points on the rim, in toward the hub, so that you will get a total of 180. Try this going spirally to the right, and then try it going spirally to the left. Now try what we call a Skipper's Spiral. This is made by starting at one of the outer-rim numbers and skipping a spoke before adding the second number in the next spoke but one, and so continuing till you get 180. This can also be done by skipping a number as well as a spoke, in forming your spiral.

There are various correct starting points; from certain ones you should go to the left spirally, and from others you must go to the right.

There are also ways—for expert skippers only—of skipping diametrically across the entire wheel. You now have visited many stopping-places; see whether you can navigate further, in your voyage around the magic wheel. There are many other points of interest, which you will discover by degrees.

How many combinations can you form to total 90, 180, 270 and 360?

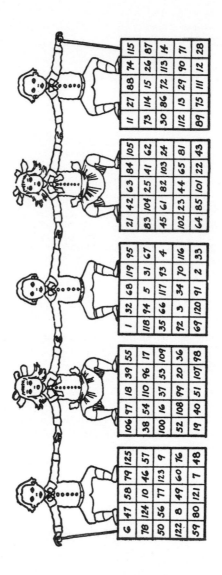

118

THE MAGIC QUINTUPLETS

These five kids were all born at exactly 3:15 A. M. Central Daylight saving time. They are known, consequently, as the 315 Quintuplets. Each one is standing on a 25-cell toy box.

If you examine all these boxes you will see that there are no two numbers alike in the entire litter. Now let's see what these kids are doing to play square with one another. For one thing they are all magic squares and each one adds up to 315.

Notice that these Quintuplets are holding hands. This is because any two of them together stand on toy boxes which add up to 630 in any number of ways. For the same reason any three of them form a total of 945, four form a total of 1260, while all five combine to make 1575.

Take any two of these kids, for example. Note that the sum of any row, column or diagonal in one of them plus the sum of any row, column or diagonal in the other totals 630. If you took three of them your total would be 945, as stated above.

There are an amazing number of combinations of 1575. If all the possible combinations were printed and you tried to copy them by hand you would have to work continuously day and night, never slowing up, for over 11,000 years to complete the job, for there are more than one billion.

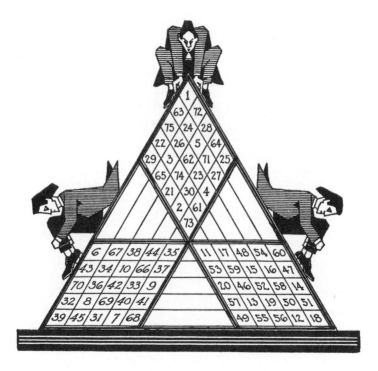

THE THREE ACROBATS

Here are three angular acrobats. See if you can do what they can. Start at the apex, hold on tight, and try.

First slide down any row on the right side or crawl along the base, or climb up the left side back to where you started from. It makes no difference, *any* of these paths will give you the total 380.

Now for your next exercise, try somersaulting. Start at the top diamond, running through *any strip of five cells*, then handspring to the diamond beneath, and run through *any strip of five cells;* finally, leap over to the last diamond and land on *any strip of five cells*. This will always give you a total of 570.

Suppose you started somersaulting exercises by doing a different turn every day; how many days would it take you to exhaust all the various possibilities to total 570? You will exhaust yourself before you find out. Remember you haven't been told about the Grecian Cross (the plus sign), the St. Andrews Cross (the multiplication sign) or the pan diagonals which add up to 190, using, of course, five numbers in any one of the 3 groups above.

BELIEVE IT OR NOT -:- By Ripley

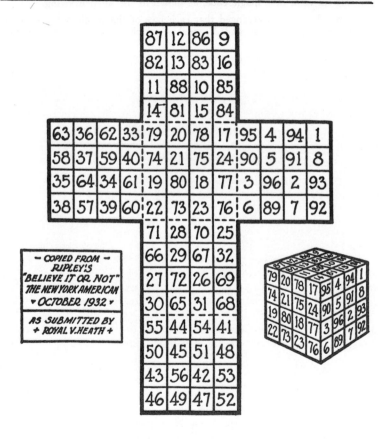

- COPIED FROM -
RIPLEY'S
"BELIEVE IT OR NOT"
THE NEW YORK AMERICAN
▾ OCTOBER 1932 ▾

AS SUBMITTED BY
+ ROYAL V. HEATH +

THE MAGIC BLOCK

The numbers on the cross, when properly folded over on the dotted line, form the six faces of a magic cube, as shown in the small drawing.

The numbers are so arranged that each face of this magic cube is a magic square, every row, column and diagonal of which adds up to 194. No number is repeated.

If you want to take a little time off see how many combinations you can form that will total 388 (twice 194). Then try 582, 776, 970, and lastly 1,164.

Suppose you decided to write out on a piece of paper all the possible combinations totaling 1,164.

You start with your first combination. You find it requires the use of 24 different numbers which, when written on a strip of paper and allowing a quarter of an inch for each number, is 6 inches long. Next to this first combination you write another combination totaling 1,164, bringing the length of the paper required to 12 inches. Continuing in this manner, how long do you suppose the paper would have to be to accommodate all possible combinations? Would you say 100 feet? 500 feet? You're wrong! Your strip of paper would be at least 700,000 miles long for there are more than 7 billion combinations possible.

If you want to copy this magic cross on a piece of cardboard and fold it on the dotted lines to make a magic cube, you can have a lot of fun with it.

Before you do this trick refer to any book that happens to be handy. Look at the first line on the ninth page, and copy the fourth word. Write this down on a piece of paper, fold the paper, and, without allowing your friend to look at it, give it to him to put in his pocket.

Then give him the magic cube. Tell him to add up any row or column on any face of the cube. When he has done this, hand him the book and tell him that the first digit of his result represents a line, the second digit represents the page, and the last digit represents the word on that line on that page. Have him look this up and write the details down on a piece of paper.

As soon as he has done this tell him to compare it with the word on the folded piece of paper you have given him.

The explanation is extremely simple. You selected the first line of the ninth page and copied the fourth word. This is obviously the number 194. Inasmuch as every row and column on the magic cube adds up to 194 (which, of course, your friend does not know) he will have to select the same word that you did.

METHOD OF DETERMINING THE DAY ON WHICH ANY DATE FALLS

Take the last two digits of the year. Add ¼ of this to it (disregarding fractions). Add the month number of Table A. Add the day. Add the year number of Table B. Divide by 7 and refer remainder to Table C.

Table A

The Month

Jan.	Add 1	leap year 0
Feb.	Add 4	leap year 3
Mar.	Add 4	
April	Add 0	
May	Add 2	
June	Add 5	
July	Add 0	
Aug.	Add 3	
Sept.	Add 6	
Oct.	Add 1	
Nov.	Add 4	
Dec.	Add 6	

Table B

The Year

	1900 to 2000	Add 0
	1800 to 1900	Add 2
9/14	1752 to 1800	Add 4
	1700 to 1752 9/2	Add 1
	1600 to 1700	Add 2
Add 1 for each century you go back		

Table C

Sun.	Mon.	Tues.	Wed.	Thurs.
1	2	3	4	5
		Fri.	Sat.	
		6	0	

What day did August 4, 1856, fall on?

Take last two digits......	56
Take ¼ of this.........	14 (disregard all fractions
Add month (Table A)...	3 if any)
Add day	4
Add 1800-1900 (Table B)	2
	79

Divide by 7 (number of days in week) = 11 + 2. Note this remainder in Table C and you will see it is a Monday.

124

A SHORT-CUT INTEREST METHOD

Everyone should know this rule, particularly those dealing in stocks. With a little practice one will find that he can do most interest problems mentally and without the use of pencil and paper.

1. Place decimal point in the principal three places to left.
2. Multiply number of days by rate of interest.

Now if the rate multiplied by the number of days equals 36, it is exactly 1/1000 of the principal—which is the same as placing the decimal point three places to the left.

For example:

Principal $1200.00, rate 6%.

Days	Rate	Rate × Days	Principal	Interest
6	6 %	36	$1200	$1.20
9	4 %	36	1200	1.20
8	4½ %	36	1200	1.20
9	8 %	72 twice 36	1200	2.40
6	3 %	18 half of 36	1200	.60
12	4½ %	54 = 1½ × 36	1200	1.80
30	6 %	180 = 5 × 36	1200	6.00

Where your rate multiplied by the days equals a fraction, for example, 7 days at 5½% would be 37½, figure 7 days at 6% which is 42 (which is $1\frac{1}{6}$ of 36 or $1\frac{1}{6}$ of the principal). This will give you the amount of interest at 6%. Now 5½% is $\frac{1}{12}$ less than 6%; therefore subtract $\frac{1}{12}$ of the 6% result *from* the 6% result. This will give you the interest for 7 days at 5½%.

RAFFLES

Suppose you sold chances for a benefit, ranging in value from 1c to 50c apiece (the value of each chance being the same as its number—chance No. 21, for example, would be 21c). What will the total of all chances amount to?

Here's the way to find out:

Suppose, as above, chances were being sold at 1c to 50c—

As the highest number is 50c, multiply the highest number by itself—50 × 50 equals...... $25.00

Multiply the lowest numbers by the highest number—1 × 50 .... .50

Divide the total by 2.................. 2 | $25.50

Result $12.75

Suppose instead of starting with the number 1, you started with the number 5, or 5c a chance to 25c a chance—

Now as there are 21 numbers multiply 21 by the highest number or 21 × 25 which equals.... $5.25

Now multiply the 21 by the lowest number, 5c, which equals 1.05

Divide the answer by 2................. 2 | $6.30

Result $3.15

FINIS

A CATALOG OF SELECTED
DOVER BOOKS
IN ALL FIELDS OF INTEREST

A CATALOG OF SELECTED DOVER
BOOKS IN ALL FIELDS OF INTEREST

CONCERNING THE SPIRITUAL IN ART, Wassily Kandinsky. Pioneering work by father of abstract art. Thoughts on color theory, nature of art. Analysis of earlier masters. 12 illustrations. 80pp. of text. 5⅜ x 8½.   23411-8

ANIMALS: 1,419 Copyright-Free Illustrations of Mammals, Birds, Fish, Insects, etc., Jim Harter (ed.). Clear wood engravings present, in extremely lifelike poses, over 1,000 species of animals. One of the most extensive pictorial sourcebooks of its kind. Captions. Index. 284pp. 9 x 12.   23766-4

CELTIC ART: The Methods of Construction, George Bain. Simple geometric techniques for making Celtic interlacements, spirals, Kells-type initials, animals, humans, etc. Over 500 illustrations. 160pp. 9 x 12. (Available in U.S. only.)   22923-8

AN ATLAS OF ANATOMY FOR ARTISTS, Fritz Schider. Most thorough reference work on art anatomy in the world. Hundreds of illustrations, including selections from works by Vesalius, Leonardo, Goya, Ingres, Michelangelo, others. 593 illustrations. 192pp. 7⅛ x 10¼.   20241-0

CELTIC HAND STROKE-BY-STROKE (Irish Half-Uncial from "The Book of Kells"): An Arthur Baker Calligraphy Manual, Arthur Baker. Complete guide to creating each letter of the alphabet in distinctive Celtic manner. Covers hand position, strokes, pens, inks, paper, more. Illustrated. 48pp. 8¼ x 11.   24336-2

EASY ORIGAMI, John Montroll. Charming collection of 32 projects (hat, cup, pelican, piano, swan, many more) specially designed for the novice origami hobbyist. Clearly illustrated easy-to-follow instructions insure that even beginning papercrafters will achieve successful results. 48pp. 8¼ x 11.   27298-2

THE COMPLETE BOOK OF BIRDHOUSE CONSTRUCTION FOR WOOD-WORKERS, Scott D. Campbell. Detailed instructions, illustrations, tables. Also data on bird habitat and instinct patterns. Bibliography. 3 tables. 63 illustrations in 15 figures. 48pp. 5¼ x 8½.   24407-5

BLOOMINGDALE'S ILLUSTRATED 1886 CATALOG: Fashions, Dry Goods and Housewares, Bloomingdale Brothers. Famed merchants' extremely rare catalog depicting about 1,700 products: clothing, housewares, firearms, dry goods, jewelry, more. Invaluable for dating, identifying vintage items. Also, copyright-free graphics for artists, designers. Co-published with Henry Ford Museum & Greenfield Village. 160pp. 8¼ x 11.   25780-0

HISTORIC COSTUME IN PICTURES, Braun & Schneider. Over 1,450 costumed figures in clearly detailed engravings–from dawn of civilization to end of 19th century. Captions. Many folk costumes. 256pp. 8⅜ x 11¾.   23150-X

STICKLEY CRAFTSMAN FURNITURE CATALOGS, Gustav Stickley and L. & J. G. Stickley. Beautiful, functional furniture in two authentic catalogs from 1910. 594 illustrations, including 277 photos, show settles, rockers, armchairs, reclining chairs, bookcases, desks, tables. 183pp. 6½ x 9¼. 23838-5

AMERICAN LOCOMOTIVES IN HISTORIC PHOTOGRAPHS: 1858 to 1949, Ron Ziel (ed.). A rare collection of 126 meticulously detailed official photographs, called "builder portraits," of American locomotives that majestically chronicle the rise of steam locomotive power in America. Introduction. Detailed captions. xi+ 129pp. 9 x 12. 27393-8

AMERICA'S LIGHTHOUSES: An Illustrated History, Francis Ross Holland, Jr. Delightfully written, profusely illustrated fact-filled survey of over 200 American lighthouses since 1716. History, anecdotes, technological advances, more. 240pp. 8 x 10¾. 25576-X

TOWARDS A NEW ARCHITECTURE, Le Corbusier. Pioneering manifesto by founder of "International School." Technical and aesthetic theories, views of industry, economics, relation of form to function, "mass-production split" and much more. Profusely illustrated. 320pp. 6⅛ x 9¼. (Available in U.S. only.) 25023-7

HOW THE OTHER HALF LIVES, Jacob Riis. Famous journalistic record, exposing poverty and degradation of New York slums around 1900, by major social reformer. 100 striking and influential photographs. 233pp. 10 x 7⅞. 22012-5

FRUIT KEY AND TWIG KEY TO TREES AND SHRUBS, William M. Harlow. One of the handiest and most widely used identification aids. Fruit key covers 120 deciduous and evergreen species; twig key 160 deciduous species. Easily used. Over 300 photographs. 126pp. 5⅜ x 8½. 20511-8

COMMON BIRD SONGS, Dr. Donald J. Borror. Songs of 60 most common U.S. birds: robins, sparrows, cardinals, bluejays, finches, more—arranged in order of increasing complexity. Up to 9 variations of songs of each species.
Cassette and manual 99911-4

ORCHIDS AS HOUSE PLANTS, Rebecca Tyson Northen. Grow cattleyas and many other kinds of orchids—in a window, in a case, or under artificial light. 63 illustrations. 148pp. 5⅜ x 8½. 23261-1

MONSTER MAZES, Dave Phillips. Masterful mazes at four levels of difficulty. Avoid deadly perils and evil creatures to find magical treasures. Solutions for all 32 exciting illustrated puzzles. 48pp. 8¼ x 11. 26005-4

MOZART'S DON GIOVANNI (DOVER OPERA LIBRETTO SERIES), Wolfgang Amadeus Mozart. Introduced and translated by Ellen H. Bleiler. Standard Italian libretto, with complete English translation. Convenient and thoroughly portable—an ideal companion for reading along with a recording or the performance itself. Introduction. List of characters. Plot summary. 121pp. 5¼ x 8½. 24944-1

TECHNICAL MANUAL AND DICTIONARY OF CLASSICAL BALLET, Gail Grant. Defines, explains, comments on steps, movements, poses and concepts. 15-page pictorial section. Basic book for student, viewer. 127pp. 5⅜ x 8½. 21843-0

THE CLARINET AND CLARINET PLAYING, David Pino. Lively, comprehensive work features suggestions about technique, musicianship, and musical interpretation, as well as guidelines for teaching, making your own reeds, and preparing for public performance. Includes an intriguing look at clarinet history. "A godsend," *The Clarinet*, Journal of the International Clarinet Society. Appendixes. 7 illus. 320pp. 5⅜ x 8½. 40270-3

HOLLYWOOD GLAMOR PORTRAITS, John Kobal (ed.). 145 photos from 1926-49. Harlow, Gable, Bogart, Bacall; 94 stars in all. Full background on photographers, technical aspects. 160pp. 8⅜ x 11¼. 23352-9

THE ANNOTATED CASEY AT THE BAT: A Collection of Ballads about the Mighty Casey/Third, Revised Edition, Martin Gardner (ed.). Amusing sequels and parodies of one of America's best-loved poems: Casey's Revenge, Why Casey Whiffed, Casey's Sister at the Bat, others. 256pp. 5⅜ x 8½. 28598-7

THE RAVEN AND OTHER FAVORITE POEMS, Edgar Allan Poe. Over 40 of the author's most memorable poems: "The Bells," "Ulalume," "Israfel," "To Helen," "The Conqueror Worm," "Eldorado," "Annabel Lee," many more. Alphabetic lists of titles and first lines. 64pp. 5$\frac{3}{16}$ x 8¼. 26685-0

PERSONAL MEMOIRS OF U. S. GRANT, Ulysses Simpson Grant. Intelligent, deeply moving firsthand account of Civil War campaigns, considered by many the finest military memoirs ever written. Includes letters, historic photographs, maps and more. 528pp. 6⅛ x 9¼. 28587-1

ANCIENT EGYPTIAN MATERIALS AND INDUSTRIES, A. Lucas and J. Harris. Fascinating, comprehensive, thoroughly documented text describes this ancient civilization's vast resources and the processes that incorporated them in daily life, including the use of animal products, building materials, cosmetics, perfumes and incense, fibers, glazed ware, glass and its manufacture, materials used in the mummification process, and much more. 544pp. 6⅛ x 9¼. (Available in U.S. only.) 40446-3

RUSSIAN STORIES/RUSSKIE RASSKAZY: A Dual-Language Book, edited by Gleb Struve. Twelve tales by such masters as Chekhov, Tolstoy, Dostoevsky, Pushkin, others. Excellent word-for-word English translations on facing pages, plus teaching and study aids, Russian/English vocabulary, biographical/critical introductions, more. 416pp. 5⅜ x 8½. 26244-8

PHILADELPHIA THEN AND NOW: 60 Sites Photographed in the Past and Present, Kenneth Finkel and Susan Oyama. Rare photographs of City Hall, Logan Square, Independence Hall, Betsy Ross House, other landmarks juxtaposed with contemporary views. Captures changing face of historic city. Introduction. Captions. 128pp. 8¼ x 11. 25790-8

AIA ARCHITECTURAL GUIDE TO NASSAU AND SUFFOLK COUNTIES, LONG ISLAND, The American Institute of Architects, Long Island Chapter, and the Society for the Preservation of Long Island Antiquities. Comprehensive, well-researched and generously illustrated volume brings to life over three centuries of Long Island's great architectural heritage. More than 240 photographs with authoritative, extensively detailed captions. 176pp. 8¼ x 11. 26946-9

NORTH AMERICAN INDIAN LIFE: Customs and Traditions of 23 Tribes, Elsie Clews Parsons (ed.). 27 fictionalized essays by noted anthropologists examine religion, customs, government, additional facets of life among the Winnebago, Crow, Zuni, Eskimo, other tribes. 480pp. 6⅛ x 9¼. 27377-6

FRANK LLOYD WRIGHT'S DANA HOUSE, Donald Hoffmann. Pictorial essay of residential masterpiece with over 160 interior and exterior photos, plans, elevations, sketches and studies. 128pp. 9¼ x 10¾. 29120-0

THE MALE AND FEMALE FIGURE IN MOTION: 60 Classic Photographic Sequences, Eadweard Muybridge. 60 true-action photographs of men and women walking, running, climbing, bending, turning, etc., reproduced from rare 19th-century masterpiece. vi + 121pp. 9 x 12. 24745-7

1001 QUESTIONS ANSWERED ABOUT THE SEASHORE, N. J. Berrill and Jacquelyn Berrill. Queries answered about dolphins, sea snails, sponges, starfish, fishes, shore birds, many others. Covers appearance, breeding, growth, feeding, much more. 305pp. 5¼ x 8¼. 23366-9

ATTRACTING BIRDS TO YOUR YARD, William J. Weber. Easy-to-follow guide offers advice on how to attract the greatest diversity of birds: birdhouses, feeders, water and waterers, much more. 96pp. 5³⁄₁₆ x 8¼. 28927-3

MEDICINAL AND OTHER USES OF NORTH AMERICAN PLANTS: A Historical Survey with Special Reference to the Eastern Indian Tribes, Charlotte Erichsen-Brown. Chronological historical citations document 500 years of usage of plants, trees, shrubs native to eastern Canada, northeastern U.S. Also complete identifying information. 343 illustrations. 544pp. 6½ x 9¼. 25951-X

STORYBOOK MAZES, Dave Phillips. 23 stories and mazes on two-page spreads: Wizard of Oz, Treasure Island, Robin Hood, etc. Solutions. 64pp. 8¼ x 11. 23628-5

AMERICAN NEGRO SONGS: 230 Folk Songs and Spirituals, Religious and Secular, John W. Work. This authoritative study traces the African influences of songs sung and played by black Americans at work, in church, and as entertainment. The author discusses the lyric significance of such songs as "Swing Low, Sweet Chariot," "John Henry," and others and offers the words and music for 230 songs. Bibliography. Index of Song Titles. 272pp. 6½ x 9¼. 40271-1

MOVIE-STAR PORTRAITS OF THE FORTIES, John Kobal (ed.). 163 glamor, studio photos of 106 stars of the 1940s: Rita Hayworth, Ava Gardner, Marlon Brando, Clark Gable, many more. 176pp. 8⅜ x 11¼. 23546-7

BENCHLEY LOST AND FOUND, Robert Benchley. Finest humor from early 30s, about pet peeves, child psychologists, post office and others. Mostly unavailable elsewhere. 73 illustrations by Peter Arno and others. 183pp. 5⅜ x 8½. 22410-4

YEKL and THE IMPORTED BRIDEGROOM AND OTHER STORIES OF YIDDISH NEW YORK, Abraham Cahan. Film Hester Street based on *Yekl* (1896). Novel, other stories among first about Jewish immigrants on N.Y.'s East Side. 240pp. 5⅜ x 8½. 22427-9

SELECTED POEMS, Walt Whitman. Generous sampling from *Leaves of Grass*. Twenty-four poems include "I Hear America Singing," "Song of the Open Road," "I Sing the Body Electric," "When Lilacs Last in the Dooryard Bloom'd," "O Captain! My Captain!"—all reprinted from an authoritative edition. Lists of titles and first lines. 128pp. 5³⁄₁₆ x 8¼. 26878-0

THE BEST TALES OF HOFFMANN, E. T. A. Hoffmann. 10 of Hoffmann's most important stories: "Nutcracker and the King of Mice," "The Golden Flowerpot," etc. 458pp. 5⅜ x 8½.　　　　21793-0

FROM FETISH TO GOD IN ANCIENT EGYPT, E. A. Wallis Budge. Rich detailed survey of Egyptian conception of "God" and gods, magic, cult of animals, Osiris, more. Also, superb English translations of hymns and legends. 240 illustrations. 545pp. 5⅜ x 8½.　　　　25803-3

FRENCH STORIES/CONTES FRANÇAIS: A Dual-Language Book, Wallace Fowlie. Ten stories by French masters, Voltaire to Camus: "Micromegas" by Voltaire; "The Atheist's Mass" by Balzac; "Minuet" by de Maupassant; "The Guest" by Camus, six more. Excellent English translations on facing pages. Also French-English vocabulary list, exercises, more. 352pp. 5⅜ x 8½.　　　　26443-2

CHICAGO AT THE TURN OF THE CENTURY IN PHOTOGRAPHS: 122 Historic Views from the Collections of the Chicago Historical Society, Larry A. Viskochil. Rare large-format prints offer detailed views of City Hall, State Street, the Loop, Hull House, Union Station, many other landmarks, circa 1904-1913. Introduction. Captions. Maps. 144pp. 9⅜ x 12¼.　　　　24656-6

OLD BROOKLYN IN EARLY PHOTOGRAPHS, 1865-1929, William Lee Younger. Luna Park, Gravesend race track, construction of Grand Army Plaza, moving of Hotel Brighton, etc. 157 previously unpublished photographs. 165pp. 8⅞ x 11¾.　　　　23587-4

THE MYTHS OF THE NORTH AMERICAN INDIANS, Lewis Spence. Rich anthology of the myths and legends of the Algonquins, Iroquois, Pawnees and Sioux, prefaced by an extensive historical and ethnological commentary. 36 illustrations. 480pp. 5⅜ x 8½.　　　　25967-6

AN ENCYCLOPEDIA OF BATTLES: Accounts of Over 1,560 Battles from 1479 B.C. to the Present, David Eggenberger. Essential details of every major battle in recorded history from the first battle of Megiddo in 1479 B.C. to Grenada in 1984. List of Battle Maps. New Appendix covering the years 1967-1984. Index. 99 illustrations. 544pp. 6½ x 9¼.　　　　24913-1

SAILING ALONE AROUND THE WORLD, Captain Joshua Slocum. First man to sail around the world, alone, in small boat. One of great feats of seamanship told in delightful manner. 67 illustrations. 294pp. 5⅜ x 8½.　　　　20326-3

ANARCHISM AND OTHER ESSAYS, Emma Goldman. Powerful, penetrating, prophetic essays on direct action, role of minorities, prison reform, puritan hypocrisy, violence, etc. 271pp. 5⅜ x 8½.　　　　22484-8

MYTHS OF THE HINDUS AND BUDDHISTS, Ananda K. Coomaraswamy and Sister Nivedita. Great stories of the epics; deeds of Krishna, Shiva, taken from puranas, Vedas, folk tales; etc. 32 illustrations. 400pp. 5⅜ x 8½.　　　　21759-0

THE TRAUMA OF BIRTH, Otto Rank. Rank's controversial thesis that anxiety neurosis is caused by profound psychological trauma which occurs at birth. 256pp. 5⅜ x 8½.　　　　27974-X

A THEOLOGICO-POLITICAL TREATISE, Benedict Spinoza. Also contains unfinished Political Treatise. Great classic on religious liberty, theory of government on common consent. R. Elwes translation. Total of 421pp. 5⅜ x 8½.　　　　20249-6

MY BONDAGE AND MY FREEDOM, Frederick Douglass. Born a slave, Douglass became outspoken force in antislavery movement. The best of Douglass' autobiographies. Graphic description of slave life. 464pp. 5⅜ x 8½.   22457-0

FOLLOWING THE EQUATOR: A Journey Around the World, Mark Twain. Fascinating humorous account of 1897 voyage to Hawaii, Australia, India, New Zealand, etc. Ironic, bemused reports on peoples, customs, climate, flora and fauna, politics, much more. 197 illustrations. 720pp. 5⅜ x 8½.   26113-1

THE PEOPLE CALLED SHAKERS, Edward D. Andrews. Definitive study of Shakers: origins, beliefs, practices, dances, social organization, furniture and crafts, etc. 33 illustrations. 351pp. 5⅜ x 8½.   21081-2

THE MYTHS OF GREECE AND ROME, H. A. Guerber. A classic of mythology, generously illustrated, long prized for its simple, graphic, accurate retelling of the principal myths of Greece and Rome, and for its commentary on their origins and significance. With 64 illustrations by Michelangelo, Raphael, Titian, Rubens, Canova, Bernini and others. 480pp. 5⅜ x 8½.   27584-1

PSYCHOLOGY OF MUSIC, Carl E. Seashore. Classic work discusses music as a medium from psychological viewpoint. Clear treatment of physical acoustics, auditory apparatus, sound perception, development of musical skills, nature of musical feeling, host of other topics. 88 figures. 408pp. 5⅜ x 8½.   21851-1

THE PHILOSOPHY OF HISTORY, Georg W. Hegel. Great classic of Western thought develops concept that history is not chance but rational process, the evolution of freedom. 457pp. 5⅜ x 8½.   20112-0

THE BOOK OF TEA, Kakuzo Okakura. Minor classic of the Orient: entertaining, charming explanation, interpretation of traditional Japanese culture in terms of tea ceremony. 94pp. 5⅜ x 8½.   20070-1

LIFE IN ANCIENT EGYPT, Adolf Erman. Fullest, most thorough, detailed older account with much not in more recent books, domestic life, religion, magic, medicine, commerce, much more. Many illustrations reproduce tomb paintings, carvings, hieroglyphs, etc. 597pp. 5⅜ x 8½.   22632-8

SUNDIALS, Their Theory and Construction, Albert Waugh. Far and away the best, most thorough coverage of ideas, mathematics concerned, types, construction, adjusting anywhere. Simple, nontechnical treatment allows even children to build several of these dials. Over 100 illustrations. 230pp. 5⅜ x 8½.   22947-5

THEORETICAL HYDRODYNAMICS, L. M. Milne-Thomson. Classic exposition of the mathematical theory of fluid motion, applicable to both hydrodynamics and aerodynamics. Over 600 exercises. 768pp. 6⅛ x 9¼.   68970-0

SONGS OF EXPERIENCE: Facsimile Reproduction with 26 Plates in Full Color, William Blake. 26 full-color plates from a rare 1826 edition. Includes "The Tyger," "London," "Holy Thursday," and other poems. Printed text of poems. 48pp. 5¼ x 7.   24636-1

OLD-TIME VIGNETTES IN FULL COLOR, Carol Belanger Grafton (ed.). Over 390 charming, often sentimental illustrations, selected from archives of Victorian graphics—pretty women posing, children playing, food, flowers, kittens and puppies, smiling cherubs, birds and butterflies, much more. All copyright-free. 48pp. 9¼ x 12¼.   27269-9

PERSPECTIVE FOR ARTISTS, Rex Vicat Cole. Depth, perspective of sky and sea, shadows, much more, not usually covered. 391 diagrams, 81 reproductions of drawings and paintings. 279pp. 5⅜ x 8½. 22487-2

DRAWING THE LIVING FIGURE, Joseph Sheppard. Innovative approach to artistic anatomy focuses on specifics of surface anatomy, rather than muscles and bones. Over 170 drawings of live models in front, back and side views, and in widely varying poses. Accompanying diagrams. 177 illustrations. Introduction. Index. 144pp. 8⅜ x11¼. 26723-7

GOTHIC AND OLD ENGLISH ALPHABETS: 100 Complete Fonts, Dan X. Solo. Add power, elegance to posters, signs, other graphics with 100 stunning copyright-free alphabets: Blackstone, Dolbey, Germania, 97 more–including many lower-case, numerals, punctuation marks. 104pp. 8⅛ x 11. 24695-7

HOW TO DO BEADWORK, Mary White. Fundamental book on craft from simple projects to five-bead chains and woven works. 106 illustrations. 142pp. 5⅜ x 8. 20697-1

THE BOOK OF WOOD CARVING, Charles Marshall Sayers. Finest book for beginners discusses fundamentals and offers 34 designs. "Absolutely first rate . . . well thought out and well executed."–E. J. Tangerman. 118pp. 7¾ x 10⅝. 23654-4

ILLUSTRATED CATALOG OF CIVIL WAR MILITARY GOODS: Union Army Weapons, Insignia, Uniform Accessories, and Other Equipment, Schuyler, Hartley, and Graham. Rare, profusely illustrated 1846 catalog includes Union Army uniform and dress regulations, arms and ammunition, coats, insignia, flags, swords, rifles, etc. 226 illustrations. 160pp. 9 x 12. 24939-5

WOMEN'S FASHIONS OF THE EARLY 1900s: An Unabridged Republication of "New York Fashions, 1909," National Cloak & Suit Co. Rare catalog of mail-order fashions documents women's and children's clothing styles shortly after the turn of the century. Captions offer full descriptions, prices. Invaluable resource for fashion, costume historians. Approximately 725 illustrations. 128pp. 8⅜ x 11¼. 27276-1

THE 1912 AND 1915 GUSTAV STICKLEY FURNITURE CATALOGS, Gustav Stickley. With over 200 detailed illustrations and descriptions, these two catalogs are essential reading and reference materials and identification guides for Stickley furniture. Captions cite materials, dimensions and prices. 112pp. 6½ x 9¼. 26676-1

EARLY AMERICAN LOCOMOTIVES, John H. White, Jr. Finest locomotive engravings from early 19th century: historical (1804–74), main-line (after 1870), special, foreign, etc. 147 plates. 142pp. 11⅜ x 8¼. 22772-3

THE TALL SHIPS OF TODAY IN PHOTOGRAPHS, Frank O. Braynard. Lavishly illustrated tribute to nearly 100 majestic contemporary sailing vessels: Amerigo Vespucci, Clearwater, Constitution, Eagle, Mayflower, Sea Cloud, Victory, many more. Authoritative captions provide statistics, background on each ship. 190 black-and-white photographs and illustrations. Introduction. 128pp. 8⅞ x 11¾. 27163-3

LITTLE BOOK OF EARLY AMERICAN CRAFTS AND TRADES, Peter Stockham (ed.). 1807 children's book explains crafts and trades: baker, hatter, cooper, potter, and many others. 23 copperplate illustrations. 140pp. 4⅝ x 6.   23336-7

VICTORIAN FASHIONS AND COSTUMES FROM HARPER'S BAZAR, 1867–1898, Stella Blum (ed.). Day costumes, evening wear, sports clothes, shoes, hats, other accessories in over 1,000 detailed engravings. 320pp. 9⅜ x 12¼. 22990-4

GUSTAV STICKLEY, THE CRAFTSMAN, Mary Ann Smith. Superb study surveys broad scope of Stickley's achievement, especially in architecture. Design philosophy, rise and fall of the Craftsman empire, descriptions and floor plans for many Craftsman houses, more. 86 black-and-white halftones. 31 line illustrations. Introduction 208pp. 6½ x 9¼.   27210-9

THE LONG ISLAND RAIL ROAD IN EARLY PHOTOGRAPHS, Ron Ziel. Over 220 rare photos, informative text document origin (1844) and development of rail service on Long Island. Vintage views of early trains, locomotives, stations, passengers, crews, much more. Captions. 8⅞ x 11¾.   26301-0

VOYAGE OF THE LIBERDADE, Joshua Slocum. Great 19th-century mariner's thrilling, first-hand account of the wreck of his ship off South America, the 35-foot boat he built from the wreckage, and its remarkable voyage home. 128pp. 5⅜ x 8½. 40022-0

TEN BOOKS ON ARCHITECTURE, Vitruvius. The most important book ever written on architecture. Early Roman aesthetics, technology, classical orders, site selection, all other aspects. Morgan translation. 331pp. 5⅜ x 8½.   20645-9

THE HUMAN FIGURE IN MOTION, Eadweard Muybridge. More than 4,500 stopped-action photos, in action series, showing undraped men, women, children jumping, lying down, throwing, sitting, wrestling, carrying, etc. 390pp. 7⅞ x 10⅝. 20204-6 Clothbd.

TREES OF THE EASTERN AND CENTRAL UNITED STATES AND CANADA, William M. Harlow. Best one-volume guide to 140 trees. Full descriptions, woodlore, range, etc. Over 600 illustrations. Handy size. 288pp. 4½ x 6⅜.   20395-6

SONGS OF WESTERN BIRDS, Dr. Donald J. Borror. Complete song and call repertoire of 60 western species, including flycatchers, juncoes, cactus wrens, many more—includes fully illustrated booklet.   Cassette and manual 99913-0

GROWING AND USING HERBS AND SPICES, Milo Miloradovich. Versatile handbook provides all the information needed for cultivation and use of all the herbs and spices available in North America. 4 illustrations. Index. Glossary. 236pp. 5⅜ x 8½. 25058-X

BIG BOOK OF MAZES AND LABYRINTHS, Walter Shepherd. 50 mazes and labyrinths in all—classical, solid, ripple, and more—in one great volume. Perfect inexpensive puzzler for clever youngsters. Full solutions. 112pp. 8⅛ x 11.   22951-3

PIANO TUNING, J. Cree Fischer. Clearest, best book for beginner, amateur. Simple repairs, raising dropped notes, tuning by easy method of flattened fifths. No previous skills needed. 4 illustrations. 201pp. 5⅜ x 8½. 23267-0

HINTS TO SINGERS, Lillian Nordica. Selecting the right teacher, developing confidence, overcoming stage fright, and many other important skills receive thoughtful discussion in this indispensible guide, written by a world-famous diva of four decades' experience. 96pp. 5⅜ x 8½. 40094-8

THE COMPLETE NONSENSE OF EDWARD LEAR, Edward Lear. All nonsense limericks, zany alphabets, Owl and Pussycat, songs, nonsense botany, etc., illustrated by Lear. Total of 320pp. 5⅜ x 8½. (Available in U.S. only.) 20167-8

VICTORIAN PARLOUR POETRY: An Annotated Anthology, Michael R. Turner. 117 gems by Longfellow, Tennyson, Browning, many lesser-known poets. "The Village Blacksmith," "Curfew Must Not Ring Tonight," "Only a Baby Small," dozens more, often difficult to find elsewhere. Index of poets, titles, first lines. xxiii + 325pp. 5⅜ x 8¼. 27044-0

DUBLINERS, James Joyce. Fifteen stories offer vivid, tightly focused observations of the lives of Dublin's poorer classes. At least one, "The Dead," is considered a masterpiece. Reprinted complete and unabridged from standard edition. 160pp. 5³⁄₁₆ x 8¼. 26870-5

GREAT WEIRD TALES: 14 Stories by Lovecraft, Blackwood, Machen and Others, S. T. Joshi (ed.). 14 spellbinding tales, including "The Sin Eater," by Fiona McLeod, "The Eye Above the Mantel," by Frank Belknap Long, as well as renowned works by R. H. Barlow, Lord Dunsany, Arthur Machen, W. C. Morrow and eight other masters of the genre. 256pp. 5⅜ x 8½. (Available in U.S. only.) 40436-6

THE BOOK OF THE SACRED MAGIC OF ABRAMELIN THE MAGE, translated by S. MacGregor Mathers. Medieval manuscript of ceremonial magic. Basic document in Aleister Crowley, Golden Dawn groups. 268pp. 5⅜ x 8½. 23211-5

NEW RUSSIAN-ENGLISH AND ENGLISH-RUSSIAN DICTIONARY, M. A. O'Brien. This is a remarkably handy Russian dictionary, containing a surprising amount of information, including over 70,000 entries. 366pp. 4½ x 6⅛. 20208-9

HISTORIC HOMES OF THE AMERICAN PRESIDENTS, Second, Revised Edition, Irvin Haas. A traveler's guide to American Presidential homes, most open to the public, depicting and describing homes occupied by every American President from George Washington to George Bush. With visiting hours, admission charges, travel routes. 175 photographs. Index. 160pp. 8¼ x 11. 26751-2

NEW YORK IN THE FORTIES, Andreas Feininger. 162 brilliant photographs by the well-known photographer, formerly with *Life* magazine. Commuters, shoppers, Times Square at night, much else from city at its peak. Captions by John von Hartz. 181pp. 9¼ x 10¾. 23585-8

INDIAN SIGN LANGUAGE, William Tomkins. Over 525 signs developed by Sioux and other tribes. Written instructions and diagrams. Also 290 pictographs. 111pp. 6⅛ x 9¼. 22029-X

ANATOMY: A Complete Guide for Artists, Joseph Sheppard. A master of figure drawing shows artists how to render human anatomy convincingly. Over 460 illustrations. 224pp. 8⅜ x 11¼. 27279-6

MEDIEVAL CALLIGRAPHY: Its History and Technique, Marc Drogin. Spirited history, comprehensive instruction manual covers 13 styles (ca. 4th century through 15th). Excellent photographs; directions for duplicating medieval techniques with modern tools. 224pp. 8⅜ x 11¼. 26142-5

DRIED FLOWERS: How to Prepare Them, Sarah Whitlock and Martha Rankin. Complete instructions on how to use silica gel, meal and borax, perlite aggregate, sand and borax, glycerine and water to create attractive permanent flower arrangements. 12 illustrations. 32pp. 5⅜ x 8½. 21802-3

EASY-TO-MAKE BIRD FEEDERS FOR WOODWORKERS, Scott D. Campbell. Detailed, simple-to-use guide for designing, constructing, caring for and using feeders. Text, illustrations for 12 classic and contemporary designs. 96pp. 5⅜ x 8½. 25847-5

SCOTTISH WONDER TALES FROM MYTH AND LEGEND, Donald A. Mackenzie. 16 lively tales tell of giants rumbling down mountainsides, of a magic wand that turns stone pillars into warriors, of gods and goddesses, evil hags, powerful forces and more. 240pp. 5⅜ x 8½. 29677-6

THE HISTORY OF UNDERCLOTHES, C. Willett Cunnington and Phyllis Cunnington. Fascinating, well-documented survey covering six centuries of English undergarments, enhanced with over 100 illustrations: 12th-century laced-up bodice, footed long drawers (1795), 19th-century bustles, 19th-century corsets for men, Victorian "bust improvers," much more. 272pp. 5⅜ x 8¼. 27124-2

ARTS AND CRAFTS FURNITURE: The Complete Brooks Catalog of 1912, Brooks Manufacturing Co. Photos and detailed descriptions of more than 150 now very collectible furniture designs from the Arts and Crafts movement depict davenports, settees, buffets, desks, tables, chairs, bedsteads, dressers and more, all built of solid, quarter-sawed oak. Invaluable for students and enthusiasts of antiques, Americana and the decorative arts. 80pp. 6½ x 9¼. 27471-3

WILBUR AND ORVILLE: A Biography of the Wright Brothers, Fred Howard. Definitive, crisply written study tells the full story of the brothers' lives and work. A vividly written biography, unparalleled in scope and color, that also captures the spirit of an extraordinary era. 560pp. 6⅛ x 9¼. 40297-5

THE ARTS OF THE SAILOR: Knotting, Splicing and Ropework, Hervey Garrett Smith. Indispensable shipboard reference covers tools, basic knots and useful hitches; handsewing and canvas work, more. Over 100 illustrations. Delightful reading for sea lovers. 256pp. 5⅜ x 8½. 26440-8

FRANK LLOYD WRIGHT'S FALLINGWATER: The House and Its History, Second, Revised Edition, Donald Hoffmann. A total revision–both in text and illustrations–of the standard document on Fallingwater, the boldest, most personal architectural statement of Wright's mature years, updated with valuable new material from the recently opened Frank Lloyd Wright Archives. "Fascinating"–*The New York Times*. 116 illustrations. 128pp. 9¼ x 10¾. 27430-6

PHOTOGRAPHIC SKETCHBOOK OF THE CIVIL WAR, Alexander Gardner. 100 photos taken on field during the Civil War. Famous shots of Manassas Harper's Ferry, Lincoln, Richmond, slave pens, etc. 244pp. 10⅝ x 8¼. 22731-6

FIVE ACRES AND INDEPENDENCE, Maurice G. Kains. Great back-to-the-land classic explains basics of self-sufficient farming. The one book to get. 95 illustrations. 397pp. 5⅜ x 8½. 20974-1

SONGS OF EASTERN BIRDS, Dr. Donald J. Borror. Songs and calls of 60 species most common to eastern U.S.: warblers, woodpeckers, flycatchers, thrushes, larks, many more in high-quality recording. Cassette and manual 99912-2

A MODERN HERBAL, Margaret Grieve. Much the fullest, most exact, most useful compilation of herbal material. Gigantic alphabetical encyclopedia, from aconite to zedoary, gives botanical information, medical properties, folklore, economic uses, much else. Indispensable to serious reader. 161 illustrations. 888pp. 6½ x 9¼. 2-vol. set. (Available in U.S. only.) Vol. I: 22798-7
Vol. II: 22799-5

HIDDEN TREASURE MAZE BOOK, Dave Phillips. Solve 34 challenging mazes accompanied by heroic tales of adventure. Evil dragons, people-eating plants, blood-thirsty giants, many more dangerous adversaries lurk at every twist and turn. 34 mazes, stories, solutions. 48pp. 8¼ x 11. 24566-7

LETTERS OF W. A. MOZART, Wolfgang A. Mozart. Remarkable letters show bawdy wit, humor, imagination, musical insights, contemporary musical world; includes some letters from Leopold Mozart. 276pp. 5⅜ x 8½. 22859-2

BASIC PRINCIPLES OF CLASSICAL BALLET, Agrippina Vaganova. Great Russian theoretician, teacher explains methods for teaching classical ballet. 118 illus-trations. 175pp. 5⅜ x 8½. 22036-2

THE JUMPING FROG, Mark Twain. Revenge edition. The original story of The Celebrated Jumping Frog of Calaveras County, a hapless French translation, and Twain's hilarious "retranslation" from the French. 12 illustrations. 66pp. 5⅜ x 8½. 22686-7

BEST REMEMBERED POEMS, Martin Gardner (ed.). The 126 poems in this superb collection of 19th- and 20th-century British and American verse range from Shelley's "To a Skylark" to the impassioned "Renascence" of Edna St. Vincent Millay and to Edward Lear's whimsical "The Owl and the Pussycat." 224pp. 5⅜ x 8½. 27165-X

COMPLETE SONNETS, William Shakespeare. Over 150 exquisite poems deal with love, friendship, the tyranny of time, beauty's evanescence, death and other themes in language of remarkable power, precision and beauty. Glossary of archaic terms. 80pp. 5³⁄₁₆ x 8¼. 26686-9

THE BATTLES THAT CHANGED HISTORY, Fletcher Pratt. Eminent historian profiles 16 crucial conflicts, ancient to modern, that changed the course of civiliza-tion. 352pp. 5⅜ x 8½. 41129-X

THE WIT AND HUMOR OF OSCAR WILDE, Alvin Redman (ed.). More than 1,000 ripostes, paradoxes, wisecracks: Work is the curse of the drinking classes; I can resist everything except temptation; etc. 258pp. 5⅜ x 8½. 20602-5

SHAKESPEARE LEXICON AND QUOTATION DICTIONARY, Alexander Schmidt. Full definitions, locations, shades of meaning in every word in plays and poems. More than 50,000 exact quotations. 1,485pp. 6½ x 9¼. 2-vol. set.
Vol. 1: 22726-X
Vol. 2: 22727-8

SELECTED POEMS, Emily Dickinson. Over 100 best-known, best-loved poems by one of America's foremost poets, reprinted from authoritative early editions. No comparable edition at this price. Index of first lines. 64pp. 5³⁄₁₆ x 8¼. 26466-1

THE INSIDIOUS DR. FU-MANCHU, Sax Rohmer. The first of the popular mystery series introduces a pair of English detectives to their archnemesis, the diabolical Dr. Fu-Manchu. Flavorful atmosphere, fast-paced action, and colorful characters enliven this classic of the genre. 208pp. 5³⁄₁₆ x 8¼. 29898-1

THE MALLEUS MALEFICARUM OF KRAMER AND SPRENGER, translated by Montague Summers. Full text of most important witchhunter's "bible," used by both Catholics and Protestants. 278pp. 6⅝ x 10. 22802-9

SPANISH STORIES/CUENTOS ESPAÑOLES: A Dual-Language Book, Angel Flores (ed.). Unique format offers 13 great stories in Spanish by Cervantes, Borges, others. Faithful English translations on facing pages. 352pp. 5⅜ x 8½. 25399-6

GARDEN CITY, LONG ISLAND, IN EARLY PHOTOGRAPHS, 1869–1919, Mildred H. Smith. Handsome treasury of 118 vintage pictures, accompanied by carefully researched captions, document the Garden City Hotel fire (1899), the Vanderbilt Cup Race (1908), the first airmail flight departing from the Nassau Boulevard Aerodrome (1911), and much more. 96pp. 8⅞ x 11¾. 40669-5

OLD QUEENS, N.Y., IN EARLY PHOTOGRAPHS, Vincent F. Seyfried and William Asadorian. Over 160 rare photographs of Maspeth, Jamaica, Jackson Heights, and other areas. Vintage views of DeWitt Clinton mansion, 1939 World's Fair and more. Captions. 192pp. 8⅞ x 11. 26358-4

CAPTURED BY THE INDIANS: 15 Firsthand Accounts, 1750-1870, Frederick Drimmer. Astounding true historical accounts of grisly torture, bloody conflicts, relentless pursuits, miraculous escapes and more, by people who lived to tell the tale. 384pp. 5⅜ x 8½. 24901-8

THE WORLD'S GREAT SPEECHES (Fourth Enlarged Edition), Lewis Copeland, Lawrence W. Lamm, and Stephen J. McKenna. Nearly 300 speeches provide public speakers with a wealth of updated quotes and inspiration—from Pericles' funeral oration and William Jennings Bryan's "Cross of Gold Speech" to Malcolm X's powerful words on the Black Revolution and Earl of Spenser's tribute to his sister, Diana, Princess of Wales. 944pp. 5⅜ x 8⅜. 40903-1

THE BOOK OF THE SWORD, Sir Richard F. Burton. Great Victorian scholar/adventurer's eloquent, erudite history of the "queen of weapons"—from prehistory to early Roman Empire. Evolution and development of early swords, variations (sabre, broadsword, cutlass, scimitar, etc.), much more. 336pp. 6⅛ x 9¼. 25434-8

AUTOBIOGRAPHY: The Story of My Experiments with Truth, Mohandas K. Gandhi. Boyhood, legal studies, purification, the growth of the Satyagraha (nonviolent protest) movement. Critical, inspiring work of the man responsible for the freedom of India. 480pp. 5⅜ x 8½. (Available in U.S. only.) 24593-4

CELTIC MYTHS AND LEGENDS, T. W. Rolleston. Masterful retelling of Irish and Welsh stories and tales. Cuchulain, King Arthur, Deirdre, the Grail, many more. First paperback edition. 58 full-page illustrations. 512pp. 5⅜ x 8½. 26507-2

THE PRINCIPLES OF PSYCHOLOGY, William James. Famous long course complete, unabridged. Stream of thought, time perception, memory, experimental methods; great work decades ahead of its time. 94 figures. 1,391pp. 5⅜ x 8½. 2-vol. set.
Vol. I: 20381-6 Vol. II: 20382-4

THE WORLD AS WILL AND REPRESENTATION, Arthur Schopenhauer. Definitive English translation of Schopenhauer's life work, correcting more than 1,000 errors, omissions in earlier translations. Translated by E. F. J. Payne. Total of 1,269pp. 5⅜ x 8½. 2-vol. set. Vol. 1: 21761-2 Vol. 2: 21762-0

MAGIC AND MYSTERY IN TIBET, Madame Alexandra David-Neel. Experiences among lamas, magicians, sages, sorcerers, Bonpa wizards. A true psychic discovery. 32 illustrations. 321pp. 5⅜ x 8½. (Available in U.S. only.) 22682-4

THE EGYPTIAN BOOK OF THE DEAD, E. A. Wallis Budge. Complete reproduction of Ani's papyrus, finest ever found. Full hieroglyphic text, interlinear transliteration, word-for-word translation, smooth translation. 533pp. 6½ x 9¼. 21866-X

MATHEMATICS FOR THE NONMATHEMATICIAN, Morris Kline. Detailed, college-level treatment of mathematics in cultural and historical context, with numerous exercises. Recommended Reading Lists. Tables. Numerous figures. 641pp. 5⅜ x 8½.
24823-2

PROBABILISTIC METHODS IN THE THEORY OF STRUCTURES, Isaac Elishakoff. Well-written introduction covers the elements of the theory of probability from two or more random variables, the reliability of such multivariable structures, the theory of random function, Monte Carlo methods of treating problems incapable of exact solution, and more. Examples. 502pp. 5⅜ x 8½. 40691-1

THE RIME OF THE ANCIENT MARINER, Gustave Doré, S. T. Coleridge. Doré's finest work; 34 plates capture moods, subtleties of poem. Flawless full-size reproductions printed on facing pages with authoritative text of poem. "Beautiful. Simply beautiful."–*Publisher's Weekly*. 77pp. 9¼ x 12. 22305-1

NORTH AMERICAN INDIAN DESIGNS FOR ARTISTS AND CRAFTSPEOPLE, Eva Wilson. Over 360 authentic copyright-free designs adapted from Navajo blankets, Hopi pottery, Sioux buffalo hides, more. Geometrics, symbolic figures, plant and animal motifs, etc. 128pp. 8⅜ x 11. (Not for sale in the United Kingdom.) 25341-4

SCULPTURE: Principles and Practice, Louis Slobodkin. Step-by-step approach to clay, plaster, metals, stone; classical and modern. 253 drawings, photos. 255pp. 8⅛ x 11.
22960-2

THE INFLUENCE OF SEA POWER UPON HISTORY, 1660–1783, A. T. Mahan. Influential classic of naval history and tactics still used as text in war colleges. First paperback edition. 4 maps. 24 battle plans. 640pp. 5⅜ x 8½. 25509-3

THE STORY OF THE TITANIC AS TOLD BY ITS SURVIVORS, Jack Winocour (ed.). What it was really like. Panic, despair, shocking inefficiency, and a little heroism. More thrilling than any fictional account. 26 illustrations. 320pp. 5⅜ x 8½.
20610-6

FAIRY AND FOLK TALES OF THE IRISH PEASANTRY, William Butler Yeats (ed.). Treasury of 64 tales from the twilight world of Celtic myth and legend: "The Soul Cages," "The Kildare Pooka," "King O'Toole and his Goose," many more. Introduction and Notes by W. B. Yeats. 352pp. 5⅜ x 8½.
26941-8

BUDDHIST MAHAYANA TEXTS, E. B. Cowell and others (eds.). Superb, accurate translations of basic documents in Mahayana Buddhism, highly important in history of religions. The Buddha-karita of Asvaghosha, Larger Sukhavativyuha, more. 448pp. 5⅜ x 8½.
25552-2

ONE TWO THREE . . . INFINITY: Facts and Speculations of Science, George Gamow. Great physicist's fascinating, readable overview of contemporary science: number theory, relativity, fourth dimension, entropy, genes, atomic structure, much more. 128 illustrations. Index. 352pp. 5⅜ x 8½.
25664-2

EXPERIMENTATION AND MEASUREMENT, W. J. Youden. Introductory manual explains laws of measurement in simple terms and offers tips for achieving accuracy and minimizing errors. Mathematics of measurement, use of instruments, experimenting with machines. 1994 edition. Foreword. Preface. Introduction. Epilogue. Selected Readings. Glossary. Index. Tables and figures. 128pp. 5⅜ x 8½.
40451-X

DALÍ ON MODERN ART: The Cuckolds of Antiquated Modern Art, Salvador Dalí. Influential painter skewers modern art and its practitioners. Outrageous evaluations of Picasso, Cézanne, Turner, more. 15 renderings of paintings discussed. 44 calligraphic decorations by Dalí. 96pp. 5⅜ x 8½. (Available in U.S. only.)
29220-7

ANTIQUE PLAYING CARDS: A Pictorial History, Henry René D'Allemagne. Over 900 elaborate, decorative images from rare playing cards (14th–20th centuries): Bacchus, death, dancing dogs, hunting scenes, royal coats of arms, players cheating, much more. 96pp. 9¼ x 12¼.
29265-7

MAKING FURNITURE MASTERPIECES: 30 Projects with Measured Drawings, Franklin H. Gottshall. Step-by-step instructions, illustrations for constructing handsome, useful pieces, among them a Sheraton desk, Chippendale chair, Spanish desk, Queen Anne table and a William and Mary dressing mirror. 224pp. 8⅛ x 11¼.
29338-6

THE FOSSIL BOOK: A Record of Prehistoric Life, Patricia V. Rich et al. Profusely illustrated definitive guide covers everything from single-celled organisms and dinosaurs to birds and mammals and the interplay between climate and man. Over 1,500 illustrations. 760pp. 7½ x 10⅛.
29371-8